Edmund Armitage Hardy, William Ridgway

Our Horses

Anecdotes from Personal Experience of Individual Horses

Edmund Armitage Hardy, William Ridgway

Our Horses
Anecdotes from Personal Experience of Individual Horses

ISBN/EAN: 9783744670579

Printed in Europe, USA, Canada, Australia, Japan

Cover: Foto ©ninafisch / pixelio.de

More available books at **www.hansebooks.com**

OUR HORSES:

BEING

ANECDOTES FROM PERSONAL EXPERIENCE

OF

INDIVIDUAL HORSES;

WITH

BRIEF PRACTICAL HINTS ON BREEDING, BUYING AND
SELLING, BREAKING, SHOEING, DOCTORING, &c.

BY

COLONEL E. A. HARDY,

RETIRED LIST, 21ST HUSSARS.

"Forasmuch as it hath happened to us to be long engaged about
"horses, we consider that we have acquired some knowledge of horse-
"manship; we desire also to intimate to the younger portion of our
"friends how we think they may bestow their attention on horses to the
"best advantage."—*Xenophon.* Περί Ἱππικῆς.

LONDON:
WILLIAM RIDGWAY, 169, PICCADILLY. W.
1878.

PREFACE.

I AM told I must have a preface, but I should not have thought it needed for a booklet like this. The title-page tells what I want to say; and I adopt the opening sentence of old Xenophon's treatise "On Horsemanship" as my apology for saying it. I may add, however, by way of further apology, that I was really much encouraged by a sort of rebuff from an eminent publisher, who told me he had "*a perfect horror of all horsey books.*" This at once set me thinking of the numbers of men and women having a thorough fondness for horses, but who, like the worthy publisher—and for that matter like myself—simply detest "horsey" language, manners, or morals. I submit, however, that there is no necessary connection whatever between the noble animal and the objectionable epithet; and it is from among the large number of those who are really and truly fond of horses, but who are in no way "horsey" folk, that I venture to look for a kindly reception of my small book. It has been to me a very pleasant little bit of writing, and I hope it may not be found unpleasant, nor altogether useless, reading.

E. A. H.

CONTENTS.

	PAGE

PART I.

INTRODUCTION.

Major.—Caliph.—Rugby.—Capilet.—Redclyffe.—St. George.—Pearl 1

PART II.

CHAPTER I.

Breeding.—Sires.—Does the present system of racing improve the breed? — Suggestions for reforming the present system of racing.—Table of pedigrees of Derby winners; etc. 36

CHAPTER II.

Breaking.—Teaching tricks.—Curing tricks.—Buck-jumpers; etc. 48

CHAPTER III.

Saddlery and harness.—Saddles.—Girths.—Bits.—Ladies' saddles.—Protest against blinkers and bearing-reins.—Fitting of harness.—Receipt for dressing leather.—Clothing; etc. 63

CONTENTS.

CHAPTER IV.

Buying and selling.—Hints for inspecting and choosing.—Points to be especially noted.—What is unsoundness?—Caution as to advertisements.—Cure for wind-sucking; etc. 77

CHAPTER V.

Shoeing.—"Goodenough, Charlier," and "Fitzwygram" shoes.—Proper method of preparing the foot for the shoe.—Clips and calkins.—Remedy for "brushing" or "clicking;" etc. 87

CHAPTER VI.

Treatment of diseases.—How to distinguish lameness.—Fomentations and cold bandages.—Poultices.—Cough.—Gripes or colic; how distinguished from inflammation of the lungs, of the bowels, and of the kidneys.—Sore back and girth-gall.—Cracked or greasy heels.—Thrush.—Sand-crack.—Corns.—Mange.—Lampas.—Sores.—Physicking.—Treatment of a tired horse.—Bleeding.—Rowels and setons.—Firing and blistering.—Construction of stables.—Run at grass; etc. 92

OUR HORSES.

INTRODUCTION.

Most of us have, I suppose, read Dr. John Brown's Notes on "Our Dogs" in his *Horæ Subsecivæ*. I do not wish to be thought as presuming to imitate, far less to rival, those most delightfully written notes, but I do wish very much to say something about "our horses," especially about Arab horses, which have, I think, of late been very unfairly underrated, but of whose value, and as sires, I have a very high opinion still. A really good specimen of the Arab horse is very seldom to be seen in England. The best one of its kind I have lately seen is a light iron-grey with dark points, ridden by a lady in the Park; but he is merely a very nice lady's-riding horse. The two brought over from India, and kindly exhibited at the Islington Horse Show, by the Prince of Wales, were certainly high-caste Arabs, but they were by no means good specimens of the breed. They were very pretty, had the true Arab head, and all that, but were far too deficient in power to give at all a correct idea of the horse a really good Arab ought to be and is. The bay, though not the handsomest, was the better of the two; the chesnut, beautiful as was his head and thoroughbred as he was all over, was too leggy (not at all an Arab characteristic), too slight in the carcase, too narrow, too deficient in muscle, to be at all a good or fair specimen of his breed. As racers, Arabs cannot compete with English or Colonial thoroughbreds; they have not the size or stride for it; and it is foolish to bring them from India, as several have been brought, to run and invariably to be beaten at Goodwood. But putting aside all the old romantic stories and poetical exaggerations, a really good Arab is a really good horse; and except for very big men and very heavy weights, he is a delightful horse to ride, to drive, and to possess. There are of course Arabs and Arabs. There is a chubby-made, bad shouldered, under-limbed animal that cannot walk well, or trot, or jump; but he is always fat, has a prettyish head, a good eye, will canter as long as you please at six miles an hour, and was beyond all doubt born in Arabia. The owner pronounces him to be a "real Arab," the owner's wife calls him "such a darling Arab;" while you, if lately arrived from England, and if you have had anything to do with horses, will probably consider the pet paraded for your inspection to be a useless little brute that can apparently do nothing a horse is meant to do, unless it is to eat bread out of your hand. But this, though common enough, is no more the correct type of the thoroughbred Arab, than the majority of horses in England are of the thoroughbred English horse. The correct type of the thoroughbred Arab is that of the best English thoroughbred English horse in miniature, with all his good points exaggerated, so to speak; the proportionate measurements being actually much in favour of the smaller horse. The fine painting of "Gang Forward," lately at the Royal Academy, would really have done exactly for the picture of a chestnut Arab of my own; and several of our best thoroughbreds—"Blair Athol" for one—when out of training, are as like the best Arabs as can be, on a large scale. I think, too, that, generally speaking, horses are not given nearly enough credit for intelligence, or for their power of personal attachment, by the majority of horse-owners, not excluding good sportsmen; and I want to show what a deal of character these noble animals possess, and to try to gain for them a somewhat more generous and sympathizing treatment as friends and companions as well as servants.

Readers of George Borrow's books will remember his theory of there being a certain mysterious species of sympathy between certain men and certain animals; his mention of a man who had a wonderful power over snakes in this way, and of his own power over horses and dogs. I am a firm believer in this theory, despite

1 *

the scientific scepticism of such high authorities as Professor Owen and others; having as I believe seen many instances of this specific power or sympathy, instances which could not be explained away. And I believe myself to have certainly possessed this power in some degree with horses, and in a lesser but still decided degree with dogs. Let me mention an instance or two to justify my belief. When I was a boy I could saddle without any difficulty a little grey mare which neither my father, an old Horse Artillery officer, nor the groom could saddle without the greatest possible trouble. She would actually sometimes throw herself on the ground in her stall, and it became a regular worrying business to saddle her for my father's ride. I found one day by some accident that I could saddle her for myself without any trouble whatever, and she never gave me any trouble afterwards. My father was very ill in bed at the time, and I well remember my dear mother's delight at having my little bit of good news about "Alice Grey" to tell him.

A very beautiful little brown mare, nearly thoroughbred, well known to be most troublesome to mount and tricksy to ride, was lent to me to ride to the shooting-ground one fine morning in September. I was told nothing of her trickiness, and I believe it was slyly hoped the Cavalry man might have the laugh against him and be promoted to a "field" officer. I went up in all innocence with my gun in my hand to the mare, as she was twisting round and round in the groom's hands, stroked her face and patted her neck, and she stood perfectly steady for me to mount, and started and carried me as pleasantly and quietly as a creature could.

I was once at an auction sale of an Artillery officer's property, when a very fine old grey charger was led out for sale. I had been told he had become very vicious, and that he had not been saddled or ridden for weeks; and on this occasion he kicked out so violently and viciously at every one attempting to go near him, and so absolutely refused to be mounted, that no one would make a bid for him. As there was no chance of his being sold, at any rate anywhere in the neighbourhood, the officer superintending the sale agreed to accept a very low sum which I offered, and I sent for the horse. I told my man to take saddle and bridle with him, to saddle the horse as he best could, and to lead him straight home; that I should meet him on the road, but he was to take no notice of me, nor stop until I touched him. After allowing due time, I strolled up the road with a bit of lucern in my hand, and soon saw my man coming with the horse as ordered; I went straight up to him, gave him my bit of lucern, without any pause or hesitation quietly put my hand on his mane and my foot in the stirrup, mounted and rode on; no kicking, all as pleasant as possible; and from that day never did "C.B." give me any trouble whatever. Without any pretensions whatever to being anything but a very ordinary horseman, I have over and over again ridden with ease, and made to do what I wanted without difficulty, horses that were most troublesome and almost unmanageable at times in other, albeit presumably much better, hands. And it is a secret source of grief to me now-a-days to find, that as my nerve as a horseman has diminished, this power over horses has diminished, if not altogether vanished, too.

I think no one who saw and attentively watched Van Amburgh with his lions, or who has seen Mr. Rarey's exhibitions of horse-breaking, could help coming to the conclusion that there was unquestionably a certain special personal sympathetic power beyond and above natural courage or acquired knack, indispensable as these qualifications are. We know that certain specific antipathies are beyond all doubt or question occasionally met with; why should we doubt that there are certain specific sympathies?

I have known an officer of proved courage, and distinguished for his attainments, utterly unhinged and upset by a dog of any sort touching him. We have all read the poet Cowper's delightful account of his hares, and how they were at once attracted by some visitors, but would even scream when attempted to be touched by others. I have seen a man whom bees would not sting; when angrily attacking all around, they would simply settle and roam over the face and body of this man, who apparently had no fear or objection to them whatever, but a sort of spell for them. But, indeed, I should think it almost impertinent to dwell at all on this point, had not such an authority as Professor Owen thought it worth while—it is some years ago—to write an article on the subject of so-called Snake-Charming, which he altogether denied to be credible, and which he attempted to account for by the snake being attracted by sounds resembling the notes of birds or other noises intimating the approach or presence of their prey. But one man will be certainly bitten, and fatally, if he attempts to catch the snake when seen; while no sooner does another man begin his pipe-blowing than the snake appears, and is instantly caught with impunity. And whatever tricks may be occasionally played, there is no doubt whatever that in many cases the snake so caught is a *bonâ fide* wild snake, and with its poisonous fangs intact, as I have proved by dissection. But now to *our* horses. On getting my commission as a Cornet—Sub-Lieutenant it is called now-a-days I believe—I had to join my regiment in India, and the first horse I ever had of my own was an Arab.

"Major"

Was a very handsome nutmeg-grey, though barely 14 hands 3 inches he was high for an Arab, and when mounted and in action he looked quite a grand horse. When fresh, he was apt to caper and jump about a good deal, but he had a beautiful temper, and always knew when he was wanted to be quiet; and if I had been ill or was weak, or any way out of sorts, he at once understood it, and behaved himself to suit my mood exactly. His faults—we all have faults—were that, unless he was on his way home and after a longish ride, it was difficult to make him walk well; he was never quite as steady as a charger should be when firing was going on; and though he had a good loin and hocks, he would not or could not jump anything of a ditch properly. He jumped height beautifully, was a capital trotter and galloper, and a beautiful parade-horse and hog-hunter. It was almost startling to watch the wonderful brightness and beauty of his eye, and the tense quivering of his every nerve and vein when a cover was being beaten; it was almost difficult to sit him at times on these occasions, he seemed positively unable to contain himself, would start and bound suddenly all-fours off the ground like a creature possessed; but the instant he was let go, the instant the rush of the start was over, he settled straight to his work, and was a delightful hunter to ride—fast, bold, clever, and temperate. I remember particularly two occasions on which he distinguished himself. We were out on a hunting party in a very hilly part of Guzerat. P—, a famous hog-hunter and myself were riding together along the side of one of the little hills which were formed of big boulders of loose rocks, our horses clambering and sliding over the stones, and I said, "What can we do with our pig, old fellow, if he breaks over ground like this?" P— had just replied to me, "Ride, ride, of course, and trust to Providence!" when a loud yell from above told a hog was afoot; and there he was, sure enough, making straight up the hill right before us. Doubts as to what one was to do were solved on the moment: spurs in, and the ground over which we had just been with difficulty picking our way at a walk, we were now galloping over as if it had been a racecourse. "Major" was faster than P—'s horse, and I soon passed him; up the rocky hill, down the other side, over a lot of bad and broken ground at bottom, without a mistake of any sort or kind did my beautiful horse carry me hand over hand up to the hog, which I was able to spear twice before the rest of the party caught us up. Most of our horses were much cut about by the stones, but I do not think there were any accidents or break-downs; and how the animals managed to get along safely at speed as they did, indeed how they kept their footing at all over such ground, is a puzzle to me to this day. At another time I was out with only one other, a brother officer and dear friend, who has lately as a "Political" been ruling the district we then hunted over, after a famous large boar, to fell which had long been an object of ambition to all the hog-hunters at the station we were quartered at. He was of great size, very savage, and was said always to take an unridable line of country. A— and self luckily came upon his tracks, and suddenly out he charged from a thick clump of bushes, knocking head-over-heels a poor beater in his way, with a loud savage grunt. He made straight for a deep ravine, down the side of which he rushed by a goat-path; it was positively little more I suppose than a foot and a half wide and broken up by rain-tracks; but down it went "Major" with me straight after him at speed, as safe and true as across a level meadow. The bottom of the ravine was for some distance wide enough to ride, and the boar being very fat and blown after the sharp burst at starting, "Major" overhauled him before he got to the impracticable part, and I was able most luckily to give him an effectual stopper with the first spear, when A— came up and we soon killed him. He was an enormous boar, with $8\frac{1}{2}$-inch tushes, which were very wide and sharp as well as long, and it was a great piece of good luck our getting him. The credit was all due to "Major." This noble horse was with me always gentle as a lamb; I taught him several tricks: he would shake hands with me just as a dog does; at a little signal-pinch on his neck he would rear straight up on end, much to the astonishment of strangers; but except to his own native groom and myself he was most troublesome to handle, and would almost always knock down any one else attempting to lead him. When his own groom was out of the way, I generally had to go to the stable myself for him, or there was tolerably sure to be a row. "Major" did me excellent service for more than eight years, when I got leave to England and home, and sold him to a brother officer who had known us both long and well. Strange to say, V—, who was really a much better rider than myself, could not hit it off with "Major" at all. The old charger took to kicking so violently with him that he was forbidden henceforth to be ever ridden on parade. He was sold afterwards to a colonel commanding an Infantry regiment, but I then heard no more of him.

After all the hard work he had done for me during eight years, a deal of hard parade work, severe marching on service, and every now and then runs such as I have described after hog, with the exception of a blemish from a bad tumble he once had with me into a dry pond on the other side of a thick and high fence which he had jumped beautifully, his legs were as clean and fresh as a colt's; not a windgall, splint, or spavin; and he was as fresh and lively to ride as ever. And in all this time with the exception of the effects of the fall which I have mentioned, and a curious sort of stroke he once got when picketed out on the march from some chill, or from the land-wind as it is called, which laid him up, hardly able to move, for a fortnight, he was never sick or sorry. Surely I have a right to think and speak well of the Arab.

"Caliph"

Was another fine specimen of the Arab. For a charger, I never had or expect to have again such a horse, Arab or English; a better charger could not be. He was καλός κ' ἀγαθός—beautiful and good, all through. I got him by a piece of great good luck. He was advertised for sale as "a very handsome and powerful Arab horse, rising five, &c. &c.: price Rupees 400"—£40— a suspiciously low price for such a description. I happened, however, to know the officer to whom application was to be made, and asked him as an old friend to tell me the particulars. He told me that the horse was really all that he was described to be, but that he had been badly kicked on the fetlock by another horse on the racecourse one morning, and had been so badly treated for it afterwards that his leg looked very bad and nobody would buy him. He told me, too, that if I did not want to work the horse immediately, he thought I could not do wrong in buying him, as he was certainly a very fine Arab, and the leg seemed to be getting all right; that the horse had a slightly cross temper, but ought to make a nice charger if properly handled; and he told me the name of his owner, who had gone home to England on leave. I knew the owner to be a first-rate judge, and I knew that my correspondent would not tell me anything that could not be strictly relied upon; so I sent for "Caliph," which I was told was the horse's name, and in due time he came. He was a rich dark bay with star and one white hind pastern; beautiful head and eye, well laid muscular and lengthy shoulders, excellent legs and feet, grand back and loin; thoroughly good all over—indeed, make and shape as good and grand as could well be; except perhaps while he was in low condition some might notice a very slight droop in his quarters, and the least thing slack in his back ribs. The march of 600 miles he had to walk to my station had made him somewhat rough in coat and poor in condition, but the blemish had gone down to a lump about the size of a pigeon's egg outside his off fore-fetlock, and seemed nowise hot or tender; and on the whole I liked the look of my new arrival immensely, and we soon became very great friends. After the horse had been a week or two in my stable and had much improved in condition and appearance, one of his hind legs suddenly swelled up in a most extraordinary way; it looked almost like an elephant's leg, and was very painful. We had at the time a most skilful Veterinary Surgeon with the regiment, and he said he knew what the attack was: "weed," he called it, and confidently told me not be alarmed about it. Part of the treatment was bleeding, and as the farrier was closing with a pin the jugular vein after the ordered quantity of blood had been abstracted, the horse suddenly dropped as if he had been shot, and lay to all appearance dying. Most fortunately our excellent "Vet." looked in just at the moment, and all the night through did he stay by the horse, having his head bathed with cold water, his face fanned, his legs rubbed, and giving him doses of nitrous æther. When pinning up the vein, farriers often blow with their mouths the hairs clear from the orifice, and, though he solemnly denied it, it is tolerably certain the farrier did so on this occasion, and that he actually blew into the vein, which might of course have caused instant death. However, the horse got up early in the morning, rapidly recovered, and improved all round in the most wonderful way. By careful bandaging with a bit of lead over the lump it had gradually diminished so as to be hardly perceptible ; and my cheap purchase turned out to be everything I could possibly wish. "Caliph" was barely 14 hands 3 inches in height, but he was to all intents and purposes a large horse to ride, and a grand horse to look at. As a charger, he was simply perfect. He was afraid of nothing ; he was naturally somewhat fiery, but the greater the row the steadier he behaved. It was something touching, something really heroic, the way the high-spirited brute refused to be put out or discomposed in a crowd, under fire, or similar trial, when he knew that to be steady was the one thing needful. In the Indian Mutiny he carried me as straight as an arrow twice into a battery we had to charge through a heavy fire, although he got a very nasty daunting sort of wound in the face the first time; and after the scrimmage was over he carried me forty miles that night without a trip or stumble; standing so steady for me to scramble on him each time after I dismounted, as he saw I was wounded, although generally somewhat fidgety to mount. His end was very sad. We were under fire from a fort, and I was a little in front, anxiously looking out for my opportunity, my beautiful "Caliph" setting an excellent example of steadiness, when suddenly he reared up, dropped on his knees, plunged and struggled up again, and then the noble beast as before stood perfectly steady and still. I dismounted and found his near fore leg had been shattered to pieces by a shot below the knee. I ought to have taken my pistol from the holster and ended his suffering then and there at once. I thought of doing so, but it would have been a terrible wrench for me to do it myself. I could not well ask any one else to do it for me just then, the moment was critical, and we knew not what might happen; so I got him under the lee of a little mound luckily close by, got the saddle off him and on to my second horse, and left him with a heap of cut green corn, which happened to be near, put before him. I never saw him again. We had to move off very soon afterwards, and being in an enemy's country I could not leave any one to look after him. When part of my regiment accompanied a force to the place, some two months afterwards, when the fort was taken and, I am glad to say, razed to the ground, my brother officers kindly tried all they could to find out what had become of my beautiful horse, but without success; they heard that the rebels had managed to get him into the fort, but they could find no further trace or tidings of him. It will be believed that I mourned most truly for my noble " Caliph."

" Rugby "

Was quite a " Little Wonder" in his way. We were to get up a race-meeting at our station. A brother officer and dear friend, afterwards killed just in front of me when leading a charge of his troop against a battery in the Indian Mutiny, said to me, " Egad ! (a favourite phrase) I think I should like to have a little fling in the races; if you will be my confederate, and do all the training work, I'll join in the games." I jumped at his proposal, which suited my fancy exactly. We calculated forthwith how much we could afford to pay for horses, and to lose if unlucky; we carefully looked over the prospectus, and agreed as to what races we should go in for; and as I had a most kind old friend (now a titled general officer) in Bombay, who was reckoned one of the best judges in India, I wrote for our racers. I told my friend what we were prepared to pay for a couple of promising maiden

Arabs, and the terms of the races for which we had taken nominations; and as I was wanting a hunter at the same time, I took the opportunity of asking Colonel C—— to buy me a nag that looked like hog-hunting, if he chanced to come across one in his dealings for us. He did the commission most kindly and capitally; and in writing me a description of the horses he had bought, he said, "I hope you will like the small hunter; I think he will prove a trump; I am not sure that he is not the best of the three." Some three weeks after this there were led up to my house one morning three horses, clothed from head to tail, with their picketing gear round their necks—two bays and a little iron-grey, my hunter, "Rugby." He was only fourteen hands and half an inch, but a pocket Hercules in make; somewhat plain and even coarse at the first sight, but the more you looked at him the more you liked him. He was somewhat sleepy-looking and no show whatever about him when at rest, but he lighted up wonderfully directly he was trotted out. He had strikingly fine points almost perfect for strength and speed; a lean, high-bred, clever head, and an eye like a beautiful woman's. He took to hog-hunting at once; he turned out a trump indeed, a first-rate hunter, and a wonderful hack to shoot off. He seemed to understand and enjoy everything in the way of sport perfectly, and to be absolutely free from fear of any sort or kind. He was on two occasions severely cut by boars charging when I had failed to spear them properly; once right across the forearm down to the bone, another time a fearful gash in the hind leg; but he was never in the least daunted. I shot several leopards (or panthers, as we called them in that part of India) off his back. He would stand as steady as a rock, with his head a little to one side, handy for me to fire; not the least frightened at the scent or sight of the beast, or even at its savage growl, which scares most horses terribly; he would start off into a gallop at once on the hint to do so, if it was necessary to bolt; and would stop again at once when wanted, without fuss or fidget. He always did exactly what was right; except, by-the-bye, on *one* occasion. When stalking deer on foot he used to follow me like a dog, and never played me false but once; when he got tired, I suppose, at my long pottering, or naughtily disposed for some reason or other, and suddenly stopped behind, gave a little neigh as if to wish good-bye, and galloped straight back to our camp, some miles away. I scolded and corrected him for this on getting home, and he never played me the trick again, though I fully thought he would after having done it once. When beating cover for hog, there is often a tremendous noise of shouting, beating on drums, firing off blank cartridges, &c.; all this din, which made some horses almost frantic, "Rugby" took no notice of whatever. He would stand under me perfectly quiet and still, half asleep to all appearance, an occasional knowing twinkle of his ear, or turn of his head, just showing that he was quite wide awake notwithstanding. But the instant the signal was given that the hog had broke, and he knew he was to start, out would go his head like a greyhound's, dragging the reins through one's fingers and oneself out of the saddle almost if not looking out, and straightforward he would rush, always in the right direction, in the most determined way. He won me a great number of first spears—the object of ambition in hog-hunting—against better and bolder riders than myself; and I do not think he ever gave me a fall. I once speared three cheetahs (the hunting leopard) off his back, one after another. I was out on leave by myself, chiefly after lions. My native shekarry (game-tracker) came into my tent with an auspicious grin, just as I was finishing my breakfast, and said, "*Sahib, I think I have got the big lion for you at last to-day; I have marked a big beast under a tree about four miles off; what it is I do not know, as I could not find his tracks on the rocky ground, and would not go near for fear of disturbing him; but I have put men in trees round to watch, and now the sun is hot he is not likely to move.*" Of course we were soon on our way. I rode an old shooting pony, but "Rugby," with a hog-spear, was led in close attendance following. The country was for the most part hilly, with deep ravines, and between the little rocky hills or knolls were small patches of cultivation, with every here and there very fine trees. From one of these trees a white rag was waved as we came on, telling us all was right so far. The tree under which the lion was supposed to be lying was soon pointed out to me; it was the largest one near, and stood handsomely in the centre of the little plateau by itself, throwing a shade nearly all over the bit of land round it. Leaving the old shekarry on the high ground with my spare guns, spear, and "Rugby," with my rifle cocked, I rode my pony quietly circling round the tree. I made all the use I could of my eyes, but could only make out that there was something very large of reddish-yellow colour under the tree, probably a lion, but I could make out nothing clear enough to justify my firing. At last I got within about thirty yards' distance, and looking intently, saw, as I thought, a large beast lying at full length fast asleep, offering apparently a most lucky shot; and taking deliberate aim at what I took to be behind his shoulder, I fired. To the shot up sprang *six* cheetahs, beautiful brutes, growling and rushing over each other, one evidently severely wounded. I was really so taken aback myself, I was stupid for a moment; but before I could determine whether to fire my second barrel or to bolt, the old shekarry yelled out, "*Come quickly for your horse, they are cheetahs, you can spear them; we'll kill them all!*" In another minute I was mounted on "Rugby," spear in hand, charging after the biggest of the cheetahs, which were now bolting in different directions. I caught up the one I was after hand over hand, but suddenly the brute crouched, and faced me fiercely, exactly like a tiger waiting for his spring; I did not half like the look of him, I thought the little horse would not either, and but for the old shekarry's confident speech to me at starting, I think I should have sheered off and back for my rifle again. "Rugby," however, had no hesitation whatever: he carried me fast and fair straight at the dangerous looking brute, just as he would have done up to a hog, and I luckily sent my spear straight through behind his shoulder, turning him right over. *"Never mind him, leave him to me; there's another to the right,"* again shouted the old shekarry, who was scuttling after me as fast as he could on his pony; and almost without stopping I at once turned off "Rugby" after another, which I also speared after a short run; and then in like manner a third. The one I had wounded in the first instance by my shot under the tree had been finished off by the old shekarry with my second gun, so four out of the six were brought to bag. It was a capital morning's sport, but a very severe run for dear little "Rugby," who, however, was none the worse for it. I used to give him after severe runs like this a bottle of good ale well sweetened with sugar, and it was curious to see how kindly the little horse took his dram. Every horseman knows the trouble and fuss, generally speaking, to get a horse to take a drench; but "Rugby" used to take his dram "like a Christian." The cheetah is as large in height and length as the leopard or panther, though lighter in carcase and slighter made, and *looks* just as dangerous; but he has not the retractile claws of the feline species, and is an absolute coward. None of these attempted to charge, even after being wounded. They are, however, destructive brutes to sheep and goats, and in default will kill dogs; and it is said they will go up a tree after a peacock at roost. A brother officer soon after my feat, as I considered it, having the similar luck to come across a pack of six cheetahs, and being very well mounted, speared every one of them, by himself, and off one horse. I think, though, he must have had better ground to go over than I had.

I believe it has been doubted whether a horse will really pursue the game he is ridden after; the rider may fancy his horse is hunting as earnestly as himself, but, it is said, he will find if he drops the rein that his steed has no notion of following the game on his own account. That the horse is not a hunting animal, and would not pursue without a rider on his back, is quite true; but it is equally true beyond all doubt that he can, and frequently does, so entirely sympathize with his rider as completely to enter into the sport. Stock-drivers in Australia will tell you that their horses will turn and double with them after a stray bullock quicker than they could turn them with a bridle; and I have on several occasions owed success entirely to my horse's *head* as well as to his legs; notably so with this horse, "Rugby." I remember particularly once, when after a severe run the hog managed to gain a very thick jungle before we could catch him—we jumped the hedge, however, and into the jungle after him—there being a sort of "ride" just before us; but we had quite made up our minds to lose our hog, and that there was not the least chance of being able to ride him further then. I was on "Rugby," who suddenly stopped short and turned off to the right with me so entirely of his own accord I was as nearly as possible off him, when—behold! there was the hog, which the little horse had evidently spied, very much beat, waiting to dodge back when we had all passed. I had just time to put my spear down and luckily caught him fairly on it as he charged, and in another minute the others came, and we soon killed him to our great delight.

Another time, in the course of a hard run we came on a river which I was not sure about the hog having crossed, or whether he had turned down among the long grass on the rocky pathway which was under the steep bank we had charged down. The river was only a few yards wide, but it looked deep, and was an awkward place to drop into. "Rugby," however, had,

I have no doubt, spied the hog on the other side, and dropped himself into the water over the girths at once without hesitation; he was the next minute swimming without the slightest fear or fuss as straight and easy as if going on dry ground. It was a very short swim, he gained ground again in a few strokes; but horsemen who know the business it is to swim most horses, will appreciate the cleverness of the hunter I had under me.

We have all heard the story of the Duke of Wellington's famous horse, "Copenhagen," giving a playful kick when the Duke patted his quarters after having been on his back some seventeen (I think) hours at Waterloo. I believe my little "Rugby" was quite equal to this; he really seemed almost as inaccessible to fatigue as to fear. I remember well on one occasion we had returned to our tents after a hard run when something occurred to recall me immediately back to quarters; something too, I forget what, absolutely necessitated my taking poor little "Rugby" to ride back upon. despite the morning's work he had already; we were a good sixteen miles from home and very bad road. The little horse carried me as gaily as a bird at a hand gallop the whole way; I only drew up to a walk for a very short spell two or three times; and as I cantered down the rising ground from where the houses of our station came in sight, I patted his neck and said, "You'll soon be at home now, Rugby;"

he answered with a little sort of squeal, put down his head with a shake, and kicked up behind, as if he had just started fresh from his stable.

All sorts of good service did this grand little horse do for me, until in getting leave home to England, I sold him to a friend in the Horse Artillery who had long wanted to have him. Now comes a strange story. D——, to whom I sold "Rugby," was a bolder and better rider than myself, and a far more famous hog-hunter; but to his utter surprise and disgust he found this noted little horse, who had never known how to flinch with me in his life, *would not take him up to a hog!* He told me he could not make it out at all, but he was utterly disappointed; he could not get the horse to follow the hog truly with him; and I believe not a spear was ever taken off "Rugby's" back after he left my stable!

"CAPILET"

Was a right well-shaped and very pretty snow white Arab; his muzzle was black and so were his hoofs, but all the rest of him was pure white. He had a ticklish mouth, and had somehow been badly broken in, and I bought him cheap from my quondam confederate in the races, now my commanding officer, who found him rather troublesome to ride as a charger. I was honestly told all this, and also told that the horse had not been worked for weeks, his owner having taken a dislike to him. I fancied the look of the horse very much; I wanted a horse at the time, and the low price enabled me to gratify my fancy at once. Having been told of his bolting propensities, I thought it well to put rather a severe bit in his mouth, and took care to gather the reins well up the first time I mounted him. The instant I was in the saddle Mr. "Capilet" threw up his head, and commenced whirling round and round so fast as almost to make me giddy; but I very soon saw what it was, he was afraid of my bit and of my hands. I dropped the reins slack on his withers, and patted his neck; he stopped, and then we started again all right and kindly, perfectly knowing why we had disagreed so at once, and feeling we were not likely so to disagree again; nor did we to any extent to speak of. Some two or three times afterwards he did not pull up quite as soon as I wanted, but for years I rode him as a charger on parade, and on service, and he behaved most handsomely with me. He went famously, too, in harness, my wife often driving him by herself. He did me, however, one terribly bad turn, which even now, after an interval of long years, I can hardly recall without a shudder. This beautiful milk-white Arab, "quite a love of a horse" to look at, would not carry a lady; he would do anything but that; most strange it was, but so it was. I twice lent him at long intervals to a lady accustomed to ride all sorts of horses from childhood, and twice he ran away with her, bringing her straight home to his stable. She had, however, on each occasion some kind excuse to make for the horse's misbehaviour, and he had behaved so well for so long a time subsequently with me, and he seemed to know so well my wife, who used to feed him with bread when waiting for me at our door, that I thought it was quite safe to put her on him one day for our evening ride. We started all right and nice, and after a while proposed to canter; but the moment this commenced, "Capilet" threw up his head with an angry shake, and off he bolted. We were on an open parade ground, and I called out to my wife to pull entirely on the right rein, and bring him round. She behaved most capitally; did exactly as I told her, turned the horse round and round me, as I pulled up myself, in a circle, and at last stopped him. I ought of course to have insisted on going quietly straight home after this, and at any rate not to have trusted "Capilet" out of a walk with a lady on his back again; but we were young and foolish in those days, and after breath was recovered and all straight again, we must needs try another canter. I shall never forget the look the horse gave me as he turned round his head before throwing it up, and with an angry little snort as if to say, "You won't stop me so easily this time," off he bolted again at score before he had gone a dozen strides; and this time straight off and away towards and under a large banian tree, of which the gigantic lower boughs stood out straightly just on a level with the rider's chest! I cannot go on with what followed; I will only say that my wife in time entirely recovered from the effects of the frightful fall, and has been mercifully spared to be as ever my help and blessing still.

For a long time after this, two years I should think, "Capilet" and I could not agree at all; sometimes he would try to bolt with me; sometimes he took to stumbling with me in an extraordinary way, almost dropping on his knees, on purpose apparently, without anything to account for a stumble; in fact we did not hit it off as before together at all. At last, however, I forgave him, and he felt so; we made it up between us, and got on all right again; the bolting, stumbling, and all the rest of it entirely ceased, and thenceforth he was as pleasant a riding horse with me as before. I need hardly say however that I never trusted him with a lady again. He did a deal of hard work for me in the Indian Mutiny; and on my going home to England after that service was over, I begged my old friend, the "Vet." I have spoken of before, to accept him and give him a kind home. A most kind home he got; and on my return to India some time afterwards, I saw the old horse again in my friend's stables, looking fresh and handsome as ever, his legs as clean as a foal's, and still trotting past most others on the road. He must have been then over twenty years old at least; but except being whiter, if possible, than before, he showed no symptoms of age.

"REDCLYFFE"

Was my wife's horse; I bring him in chiefly to show it was no deficiency on her part that caused "Capilet's" bad behaviour to her. I was on the Staff at that time, and one day had been doing a lot of work in the saddle for the General, and had fairly used up my own horses for the day, when in came a note to say he wished me to ride with him all round the line of country we had fixed upon for a sham campaign. Near me lived a Mahomedan gentleman, who generally had two or three good Arabs in his stable, and who often came in to consult me on veterinary matters. He had lately been telling me of a little horse he had newly bought from a famous Arab horse-dealer in Bombay, of which he had a high opinion, and had asked me to ride and try him; so I thought this was just the opportunity, when I really wanted a mount, to send my "salaam" and say I should be happy to ride his new horse if it was convenient to send him over to me then. He was a beautiful little horse, bright bay, with a star and a little white on both hind pasterns, mane and tail quite picture fashion. My General had been a famous hog-hunter in his younger days, and was quite game for a good gallop still, and he enjoyed the larking across the country where we were to have our "Chobham."

My native friend's little horse carried me so gamely and well, I quite fell in love with him, and I determined I would buy him should fitting opportunity occur. I did buy him not long afterwards, and he soon became an especial favourite. Quite different from the ungallant "Capilet," "Redclyffe" was a perfect lady's horse. With me the little dandy would play all sorts of pranks, rear right upon end, and sometimes it took all I knew to sit him; but with his mistress he was always perfectly steady and gentle, though still always full of life and spirit. It was pretty to see the little horse galloping under her, as handsome as a picture and looking as proud and fiery as Lucifer, but perfectly under her control under all circumstances and at any pace. Of an evening, when our horses were being walked round our "compound," as it is called in India, we used often to give them a carrot if we were at home; a few carrots were cut up and put in a basket ready to take out; of course they got to know the sight of the basket right well. "Redclyffe" was privileged to be let loose on these occasions, instead of being led up as the others were. As soon as he was let go and saw what it was for, away he would dash at speed, kicking and plunging like a creature wild with spirits, then he would suddenly turn and charge straight towards where we stood, as if fiercely intent to knock us down, but when within a few yards from us he would halt himself sharp on his haunches, and trot up in the gentlest possible manner to be petted and fed. It was the prettiest bit of acting possible. When my wife had to leave me for England, I sold this dear little horse to a very light weight and capital horseman, under whom he turned out a first-rate hog-hunter, often winning spears from the big ones.

"St. George"

Was so named after the flourish of the lance thus designated in the old lance drill; I was then in a Lancer regiment. He was a grey Arab, high bred, handsome, powerful, and fast. I liked him very much, but somehow he never would like me. He was a right good horse and an excellent charger, but he was the only horse I ever had with whom I could never properly come to terms; I could never make my hands suit his mouth properly; with a light bit I could not hold him, with anything of a severe bit he would not go comfortably at all. I sold him to an old friend, P—— whom I have mentioned in a former page as a famous hog-hunter, and with him he got on capitally and became a great favourite. He had the queer, round enlarged-looking fetlocks which so caught one's eyes in the famous Derby winner " Gladiateur," but they never affected his work in the slightest degree. A very singular occurrence happened to me with this horse. Soon after he had come to me I wanted to qualify him to run for the hog-hunters' stakes in a race-meeting shortly to come off, and having got a fortnight's leave I sent him on the road to ride the last short stage to my ground; I had about forty miles of rough road to ride, and posted four or five horses and ponies to do it on. It was a fine, bright, cold-weather morning, I was in high spirits in the thoughts of my little holiday and anticipated sport, and I found "St. George," when I came to the place he was posted at, wild with spirits too. As soon as I got on him, quite forgetting how young and fresh the horse was; forgetting, too, his hot temper which I had already had experience of; in sheer exuberance of my own spirits and in sympathy with my horse's, I slapped him on the neck, pricked him with the spurs, and told him to go as fast as he liked. Off he started at score, both of us wild with spirits. About a quarter of a mile ahead of us by the roadside was a small village, and out of this village came slowly streaming along towards us a large herd of cattle, on their way to the jungle to graze for the day. Straight at this herd we dashed along almost at speed; as I expected, they quickly turned and galloped off both sides of the road, with their tails high up, off towards the fields or jungle on either side, leaving all clear for us as we came tearing on,—all but one large bullock, which whether from fierceness, or fright, or sheer stupidity, stood firm looking at us, but broadside on right across the road. I could, I fancy, have pulled up if I chose, or have pulled off the road; but, strange to say, neither I nor "St. George" seemed to have the least idea of doing anything but charge straight ahead. I have never been able to account for it, but so it was. The horse took a tremendous spring for his jump, but unfortunately too far off, and instead of clearing the bullock, as I really think he would have done but for the too long take off, he alighted exactly on his back; fore legs on one side, hind legs on the other, and over we all rolled together. I picked myself up as quickly as I could, and pulled "St. George's" fore legs from under the bullock; he soon freed himself and struggled up all right, and with hardly a scratch; but it had been too much for poor bullock; he turned up the whites of his eyes, gave a groan or two, and died then and there! I imagine his spine must have been broken by the sudden shock and weight upon it. When I came back past the same place at the end of my fortnight's leave, there was the huge skeleton of the poor beast picked clean where he lay. . . . .

People who merely get on their horses to go for their ride and get off them when they come home, without any further intercourse, can have no idea of the injustice they do to these noble animals, and the pleasure of which they deprive themselves; and I believe I have owed my life on more than one occasion—I will not say to my horse, because every horseman of any experience must be able to say that—but to the special affection of my horse for me; and I will end with a very brief notice of

"PEARL."

He was a very beautiful flea-bitten gray Arab of the highest caste, and quite a fancy horse all over. I taught him all sorts of tricks, and he knew me and what I wanted him to do as well as any dog could. One evening I got on him for my ride—he was exceedingly fresh, having not been ridden for some days; it was rather dusk, and on the side of the road there had been put some heaps of stones, or "kunkur," for repairing it. As " Pearl " got excited with his gallop, he took to bounding along half wildly across the road, and went over several of these heaps of stones; but at last at one of them, either not seeing it rightly in the dusk or missing his footing, in the course of one of his gambols his feet caught on the loose stones, and over we rolled. The horse got up instantly, and was continuing his gallop with my head on the ground and my foot in the stirrup! I had sense enough to call out to him by name to stop and be steady, and the sensible brute did stop, almost immediately, and waited perfectly steady, quietly looking round at me till I should get up. I was stunned, and the back of my head much cut, and had good cause to be grateful for the assistance given me by a kind lady who had seen the catastrophe from a distance, without whose help I should have been in a most uncomfortable plight for some time, to say the least of it. But a few strides more of my head being dragged and bumped on that hard road, as must have happened with almost any horse that did not know and care for me as this beautiful "Pearl" did, and I should certainly not have been alive to tell the story. I sold "Pearl" not long after this accident, though somewhat sorrowfully as may be supposed, to a kind master, and he subsequently won some good races. When I saw him again, nearly three years afterwards, the horse knew me perfectly when I spoke to him, and seemed quite delighted to "shake hands" with me again, as I had taught him to do, though I was assured he had never done it since he had been in his new master's possession. . . . .

CHAPTER I.

Breeding, Breaking, &c.

There are so many books, and so many good ones, too in their several ways, about the choice, treatment, and management of horses, I feel that some apology may be considered due from me for adding to their number. But I venture to hope that those who have cared to go with me so far may like to go on with me a little further, and as I have had a tolerably large experience I presume to think I have a right to ask them to do so. I cannot, of course, hope to be able to say anything absolutely new on the subject, but still I shall try to avoid as much as possible the ground that has been sufficiently beaten by others, or at least to take a somewhat different way of beating the same ground; and as I have so frequently been asked to recommend some short practical and readable manual to help friends how to buy a horse, and to treat him rightly when they have got him, and have really often had much difficulty in directing their choice satisfactorily, I hope after all I may not be thought so very presumptuous in attempting to supply what there is apparently still room for.

BREEDING.

I begin at the beginning with horse-breeding; but as this is necessarily a purely technical subject, those who do not care to go into my very brief notice of it can skip till past the table of pedigrees.

Breeding on any but the smallest scale requires so much money, such intimate knowledge of the various strains of pedigrees and their respective characteristics, and so much knowledge of horse-flesh generally, and is after all so much of a lottery, that my advice would be simply that of *Punch's* to persons about to marry, "Don't." I have, however, twice had colts of my own breeding, and they both luckily turned out just what I bred for, and what I thought I had a right to expect; and in India I had opportunities of seeing horse-breeding on a very large scale in the Government studs, the management and results of which I was able to make myself thoroughly acquainted with. I would say in the first place, whatever venture you make in the breeding line, unless you want to breed cart-horses, or Norfolk trotters, always have a thoroughbred sire. For trotters, that is the particular style of horse so-called, a trotting-mare and thoroughbred horse seldom give the required produce; for this you must have a Norfolk trotter for the sire. A well-shaped and not too heavy cart-mare will often produce a good carriage or riding-horse by a thoroughbred sire; but the chances are all against the best bred mares giving you anything likely to repay the cost and trouble from an under-bred horse. I would say, too, remember always that as a general rule "like produces like;" almost every point good or bad is more or less hereditary. The sire and dam should be sensibly selected, not put together because the horse happens to pass your way; and they should both be sound, especially in sight and wind. The extraordinary differences in Arabs, showing much quality too, is I believe attributable to their Arabian owners attaching so much importance to the side of the dam, as to be, generally speaking, comparatively indifferent what sires their mares are put to. I had in India a curious but satisfactory proof of how much the result in the produce depends on the selection and pairing of the sire and dam. At one of the great Government breeding establishments, where the sires are for the most part thoroughbreds sent from England and a very few Arabs, almost every undersized inferior colt led out for inspection was by an Arab sire; and as I was known to be a great admirer of Arabs, each miserable specimen was pointed out to me as the progeny of one of my pets. But at another of the studs the case was exactly reversed; the finest colts there were found almost invariably to be by the Arab sires! The explanation of course was that at the one place, where the officer did not fancy Arab sires, they had only the worst mares put to them; and at the other place, where they were the favourites, they had the best mares; and the produce resulted accordingly. Where a compact hardy horse like the famous "Fisherman" gets a lengthy delicately made colt, or an elegant light made horse like "Saunterer" gets a short-legged sturdy colt, it will be generally found that such exceptions can be accounted for from the side of the dam, or from a strain or two back; and it is here where an accurate knowledge of pedigrees and of their characteristic hereditary peculiarities is so essential. "Stonehenge" tells us that if we want to breed steeple-chasers or hunters we should choose the blood descended from *Sir Hercules, Defence,* The Colonel, The Saddler, Economist, *Harkaway,* Safeguard, Memnon, *Lottery, Sheet Anchor, Faugh-a-ballagh, Ratcatcher,* Monarch. And that for racers, we should choose the blood of *Touchstone,* Lancelot, *Priam,* Plenipotentiary, Velocipede, *Pantaloon,* Beiram, *Bay Middleton,* Phantom; all good sires of race-horses, but which have never produced, he tells us, a good hunter or steeple-chaser. The names I have put in italics are the sires whose blood I should myself select for choice. The same clever author tells us that for breeding purposes mares with rather drooping quarters are the best, for physical reasons; but here I venture distinctly to differ from him. For one thing, the drooping quarter is a point especially likely to be inherited, and difficult to be got rid of in breeding; and I should say unhesitatingly that, other points being equal, the straighter the spine from the withers to tail the better for all purposes. I append a table which I have drawn up in, I think, a handy form showing the immediate pedigrees of Derby winners for the last thirty years; it is interesting to note how many winners have in their turn become sires of winners; and it may be found useful as a convenient kind of short index to our best blood. A mare may with advantage be worked gently up to very near the time of her foaling; but she soon begins to show symptoms of tiring sooner as she gets heavier, and she should of course be favoured accordingly in her work. The period of gestation is almost always exactly eleven months. Shelter and a soft bed for her foal to be dropped on are all the help the mare needs in the great majority of cases; if the foal is very weakly at first, it should be helped to stand on its legs to suck; and take care that there are no holes for mother or foal to slip into, or bars between which a leg may be caught. It is most strange how very careless some owners of valuable stock can be in overlooking these most ordinary precautions. I have seen the unclenched point of a large nail sticking out from the paling, just the thing to wound a colt at play, possibly tear his eye out: I have seen a thoroughbred mare left to foal in a meadow where the only watering-place was a steep slippery banked ditch, into which I heard (not at all to my surprise) she rolled one night, after the pains of foaling had come on, and was drowned. Mr. Tattersall's breeding paddocks at Kilburn were models of all that was comfortable and safe in this respect; it was one of my treats about town some thirty years ago to spend an afternoon in looking over the beautiful blood sires, dams, and their produce at that most admirably arranged establishment. If the mare has been all along accustomed to oats, she should have about half the usual quantity of corn the first few days after foaling, but plenty of gruel and bran mash as well as green food. If she is wanted to go on breeding, the books and breeders say take her to the horse the tenth day after foaling; and if you keep your mare solely for breeding this is perhaps the best rule. But otherwise, no creature in any way intended to take part in the usual work of life should be expected to nourish an offspring from the breast and another in the womb at the same time; and the foal should be weaned before pregnancy is again allowed to take place. Five months or so is quite old enough for weaning, if wanted; and foals soon get into the way of drinking cows' milk if it is advisable to help their nursing in this way, as it often may be from the first.

And now before coming to my table of pedigrees of thoroughbred horses at the end of this chapter, I would like to stop for a moment's consideration of the question as to the effects of racing on our breed of horses about which so much anxiety prevails, and most justly prevails, at the present time. Is racing the chief cause which has produced and still continues our famous breed of horses, or is it gradually ruining the source of our breed and beginning to produce more bad ones than good? The question is really a very difficult one to answer. One sees a large number, the large majority indeed by far, of young thoroughbreds, weedy, slight made, straight-shouldered, crooked-legged creatures that cannot carry above eight stone or gallop with it beyond half a mile, and are broken down either in wind or limb before they are four years old, and one is told such is the fruit of racing. "How," it is asked, "are you to expect the continuance of an efficient breed of horses when people are tempted to work the young things at one year old, and race them at two years old; when the weights and distances suitable under such circumstances are necessarily so small that the race is no test or requirement of strength or endurance, but simply of speed for a spurt of half a mile; when consequently the career of most of your racing stock is over and done with before they have come to anything like their proper maturity of powers?" And the question thus put would seem to answer itself. But on the other hand, it is quite certain that it has been to racing that we owe the existence of our famous breed of horses; it is certain, too, that the weediness and weakness complained of in so many of our young thoroughbreds arise much more from injudicious breeding than from injudicious racing, which, after the Spartan fashion, kills off the young creatures not strong enough to stand it; and when one sees the beautiful power and proportions which on the whole generally are to be seen and are essential in the winners of our great races, most of whom have commenced their running at two years old; when one hears of breeders, solely in consequence of racing, getting as much as 2000 guineas for a yearling, and thinks what an enormous encouragement and stimulus the chance of such a price must be for the carrying on and perfecting the breed, the advantage of upholding racing as a national institution would seem clearly proved. As noticed before, it may be urged in favour of early training and racing that only the strong ones can stand it; and no one can form a correct idea of the thoroughbred race-horse simply from seeing him in his training form, one must see him when he has retired into private life as it were, and has assumed his proper comely proportions. Blair Athol, who won one of the fastest Derbys on record, and afterwards the St. Leger, looks, and is, equally fit to be a magnificent weight-carrying hunter or charger; and the same may be said of King Tom, General Peel, Scottish Chief, Craig Millar, Doncaster, and many others, indeed the majority of really proved good race-horses. But still the victories obtained of late years by foreign horses over the longer courses, which must be put down simply to the more favourable conditions under which they have been previously trained to compete, seem to point to something certainly wrong in our present system. Some improvements have certainly been made of late by the Jockey Club in the rules of racing, especially in limiting the time when races may be run to from 25th March to 15th November in each year; but this open time should be further limited still. From 1st April to 1st November would be ample time for all races worthy of the name, and three weeks more of close time would be of the greatest advantage to our race-horses. Then again, the whole system of handicaps should be abolished, or at least very greatly modified. This system is the greatest stumbling-block and does more harm directly and indirectly, physically as regards our horses, morally as regards our men, than anything else on the turf. Certain fair and reasonable extra weights should be accorded to winners of certain races, so that the chances of winning prizes should not be entirely confined to a few stars; but the system of a general handicapping for each season, with weights varying in some cases as much as three stone, is altogether mischievous and unjustifiable. It is unfair on the really sporting and honest owners of good horses to penalize them by such enormously differing weights down to the level of bad ones; it is a great temptation to the less honest owners of either good or bad horses to run them under false orders, so as to get them favourably handicapped; it increases the number of trumpery and purely speculative meetings to a most prejudicial degree; and it is the chief foundation and support of the "ring," of the professional gambling among a set of people, the great majority of whom know and care nothing about horses, except as mere names or counters to make betting "books" upon, which is the great curse of racing. And in this connection I cannot help, in defiance of many a smile or sneer that may be excited by my proposition, expressing my very earnest wish and hope that a hint may be given by the police authorities of the illegality of Tattersall's subscription betting-room, which most assuredly ought in all equity not to be tolerated while "publicans" are being continually and rigidly punished for permitting betting on their premises. If racing is, as is argued by its best and ablest supporters, the *fons et origo* of the noble breed of horses we have so long and so justly been famous for all the world over, we should surely do all that in us lies to purify the fountain. Let it be a pursuit and amusement for all true and upright sportsmen who can afford it, freed as far as possible from all scandal or reproach; arrange, so far as is practicable by arrangement, that the prizes must be competed for by horses of a stamp whose breed is worth upholding, not creatures who cannot gallop over half a mile nor carry more than a feather-weight; and protect as much as possible the rising generation of thoroughbred sires and dams from being run off their legs when only two or three years old, and their progeny from the inevitable consequences of such cruelly premature exhaustion and decay. . . . . . .

IMMEDIATE PEDIGREES OF DERBY WINNERS FROM 1848 TO 1878 INCLUSIVE.

Derby Year.	Winner.	Pedigree of Winner.		Pedigree of Winner's Sire.		Pedigree of Winner's Dam.		Remarks.
		Sire.	Dam.	Sire.	Dam.	Sire.	Dam.	
1848	Surplice (*a*)	Touchstone	Crucifix	Camel	Banter	Priam	Octaviana	(*a*) Won the Leger
1849	Flying Dutchman (*a*)	Bay Middleton	Barbelle	Sultan	Cobweb	Sandbeck	Darioletta	Ditto.
1850	Voltigeur (*a*)	Voltaire	Martha Lynn					Ditto.
1851	Teddington	Orlando	Miss Twickenham	Blacklock	Mare by Phantom	Mulatto	Leda	
1852	Dan O'Rourke	Irish Birdcatcher	Forget-me-not	Touchstone	Vulture	Rockingham	Electress	
1853	West Australian	Melbourne	Mowerina	Sir Hercules	Guccioli	Hetman Platoff	Oblivion	(*b*) Won the St Leger & 2000 Gs
				Humphrey Clinker.	Mare by Cervantes.	Touchstone	Emma	
1854	Andover	Bay Middleton	Sister to Ægis	Sultan	Cobweb	Defence	Soldier's Joy	
1855	Wild Dayrell	Ion	Ellen Middleton	Cain	Margaret	Bay Middleton	Myrrha	
1856	Ellington	Flying Dutchman	Ellerdale	Bay Middleton	Barbelle	Lanercost	Mare by Tomboy	
1857	Blink Bonny (*c*)	Melbourne	Queen Mary	Humphrey Clinker.	Mare by Cervantes.	Gladiator	Mare by Plenipotentiary, out of Myrrha.	(*c*) Won the Oaks.
1858	Bendsman	Weatherbit	Mendicant	Sheet Anchor	Miss Letty	Touchstone	Lady Carew	
1859	Musjid	Newminster	Peggy	Touchstone	Beeswing	Muley Moloch	Fanny	
1860	Thormanby	Melbourne, or Windhound.	Alice Hawthorne	Humphrey Clinker, or Pantaloon	Mare by Cervantes.	Muley Moloch	Rebecca	
1861	Kettledrum	Rataplan	Hybla	The Baron	Pocahontas	The Provost	Otisina	
1862	Caractacus	Kingston	Defenceless	Venison	Queen Anne	Defence	Mare by Cain	
1863	Macaroni (*d*)	Sweetmeat	Jocose	Gladiator	Lollipop	Pantaloon	Banter	(*d*) Won the 2000
1864	Blair Athol (*e*)	Stockwell	Blink Bonny	The Baron	Pocahontas	Melbourne	Queen Mary	(*e*) Won the Leger.
1865	Gladiateur (*f*)	Monarque	Miss Gladiator	Sting, or The Emperor, or The Baron.	Poetess	Gladiator	Tuffrail	(*f*) Won the Leger and 2000 Gs.
1866	Lord Lyon (*g*)	Stockwell	Paradigm	The Baron	Pocahontas	Paragon	Ellen Horne	(*g*) Won the Leger
1867	Hermit	Newminster	Seclusion	Touchstone	Beeswing	Tadmor	Miss Sellon	
1868	Blue Gown	Beadsman	Bas Bleu	Weatherbit	Mendicant	Stockwell	Vexation	
1869	Pretender (*h*)	Adventurer	Ferina	Newminster	Palma	Venison	Partiality	(*h*) Won the 2000
1870	Kingcraft	King Tom	Woodcraft	Harkaway	Pocahontas	Voltigeur	Wedding-day	
1871	Favonius	Parmesan	Zephyr	Sweetmeat	Gruyère	King Tom	Meutmore Lass	
1872	Cremorne	Parmesan	Rigolboche	Sweetmeat	Gruyère	Rataplan	Mare by Gardham	
1873	Doncaster	Stockwell	Marigold	The Baron	Pocahontas	Teddington	Sister to Singapore.	
1874	George Frederick	Marsyas	Princess of Wales	Orlando	Malibran	Stockwell	The Bloomer	
1875	Galopin	Vedette	Brown Duchess	Voltigeur	Mare by Birdcatcher.	Flying Dutchman.	Espoir	
1876	Kisber	Buccaneer	Mineral	Wild Dayrell	Mare by Little Red Rover	Rataplan	Manganese	
1877	Silvio (*i*)	Blair Athol	Silverhair	Stockwell	Blink Bonny	Kingston	England's Beauty	(*i*) Won the Leger
1878	Sefton	Speculum.	Mare by West Australian, out of Clarissa.	Vedette	Doralice	West Australian	Clarissa	

CHAPTER II.

Breaking.

Breaking-in as practised in my younger days, excepting of course with thoroughbred horses, generally commenced by putting an enormously thick and heavy snaffle into the colt's mouth, this was reined up as tightly as his poor neck would allow to a surcingle; a heavy caveson, with goodness knows how many straps and buckles, was then put on, and thus accoutred the colt was led out in the public road, a second man following behind with a long cracking whip. We have, I hope, improved a good deal upon this now; but I still see the things called "mouthing bits" constantly used, than which heavy masses of iron nothing can well be worse or more teasing for a fine mouth. The best bit to begin with is a perfectly smooth snaffle, about the thickness of the middle joint of an average sized middle finger; instead of the tight reining up, the reins should merely feel the mouth, and prevent the colt getting his head right down as they sometimes will, no more than that; and it is a good plan at first to pass them through a plain running ring, which helps to keep his head straight. The caveson,

BREAKING.

properly made and fitted, I should always use still for the first lessons; it is the best possible help in the first instance for teaching obedience, proper paces, jumping, &c. Lead the colt round at a walk first once or twice, then lengthen the caveson rope gradually, and get him to trot, saying "trot," and just showing him your whip; if he is very wild you should have an assistant to help you, and prevent his breaking away out of the circle, but it is far better to do without any one but yourself if you can. After he has settled down a little and got to trot round pretty kindly, say "halt," and quietly pull him into you in the centre of the circle, make much of him, and reward him with a bit of carrot or something from your pocket; then start him round again the reverse way. After a few lessons make him break into a canter from the trot on the word "canter;" and at the halt, stand in front of him, and, taking a ring of the snaffle in each hand, make him go back, saying "rein back;" standing on his near side and touching him gently with the end of your whip on his left side where you would spur, make him sidle towards the right, without advancing, saying "right pass;" then put yourself on his off side, and in the same way make him go "left pass;" then standing facing him again as before, say "forward," and walking backwards yourself lead him up into the centre of your circle, and reward him. The caveson is generally made too heavy and with an unnecessary number of straps about it; but it must of course be strong enough to prevent all risk of breaking; and the noseband, in which the whole conquering power of the cavezon consists, should be carefully padded so as to allow of being buckled tolerably tight without galling. For all the first lessons get to an absolutely quiet place, where there is nothing whatever to distract attention; let the lessons be short, say half-an-hour at a time; if you can, give three lessons in the day; but on no account in the early lessons leave a day entirely blank; always have bits of carrot, or lucern, or sugar and oats in your pocket to reward with; and if possible be alone. If the horse is very fresh and unmanageable, it is best to starve him a little; a fast without food or water for from twelve to twenty-four hours is a wonderful quieter, and makes him very grateful for anything given by hand. I would not of course starve a horse as a part of his breaking generally, only in exceptional cases, and under particular circumstances; but I have known horses plunge about so wildly while being lunged when they were fresh as to injure themselves severely; and I remember a case of a valuable colt which died from a ruptured diaphragm in this way. For the first mounted lessons repeat at first as nearly as may be what you made the horse do with the caveson just to begin with, then ride him round a field instead of the confined circle, and then take him on the road. The system practised in our Cavalry is the best possible, if it were not generally so absurdly overdone; the horses and men are too often kept doing the same things over and over again till they are all sulky and sick of the whole business; the horses are too often so rigidly taught to go "collected," as riding-masters lovingly call it, that their only idea of galloping out when pressed to speed, as when wanted in a charge, is running away. But the circling, turning short to right and left, passaging, and reining back, practised with moderation and judgment, much as I have tried to lay down in the lessons I have suggested, first with the caveson, then when mounted, add exceedingly to the pleasantness of a horse for riding. Then as you have time and inclination, go on with him, teaching him to jump, gallop at speed and stop when wanted, turn to right or left by a simple signal of turning your whip over to the right or to the left, face firing, stand steady to music—make him, in short, a perfect mannered horse. After a while, if you want to make him a clever horse across country, put him on a pair of good knee-caps, and lunge him gently over heaps of stones, loose bricks, fallen bits of timber, ditches, &c.; it is wonderful how safe and clever a horse becomes with a little preparatory practice of this kind. Sir Francis Head, in his pleasant book, "The Horse and his Rider," recommends riding a young horse over ground of the above description to make him a clever hunter;

but I am inclined to think he never tried this himself: I have; and though then not much troubled as to nerves, I must say I decidedly prefer beginning this sort of instruction with the caveson, just at first. Begin your mounted lessons with blunt spurs; sharp spurs are very apt make a horse angry, and nothing delays the breaking-in so much as loss of temper on either side.

For harness, the horse having of course been broken previously into hand and saddle, begin at first by simply exercising him with harness on; then let him have to pull against a man holding on to long traces; then a log of wood, or bush harrow. Then put him alongside a steady old horse in a break, and if properly handled, he will in most instances very soon learn his business after a few driving lessons. If you cannot get the great advantage of a break horse, put your pupil into a butcher's cart or similar vehicle; taking care of course to do it very quietly—no rude banging the shafts against his quarters, or similar provocative. Get him first to lead quietly in harness, practising turning a corner or two, and up and down a hill; then drive him. Much time is really saved in the end by this gradual way of working, slow as the description of it may appear. Short and simple but frequent lessons to begin with, always leaving off when well done, but never leaving off till well done, a reward always ready in your pocket to give on the spot, absolute temper and patience, and for the very first lessons absolute privacy if possible, are the chief secrets and essentials for teaching a horse speedily and well. All horses, except race-horses, should, I think, be broken in for harness, it adds so immensely to their usefulness; and being driven with good hands occasionally in a not heavy carriage in no way hurts a horse for riding, whatever fastidious horsemen say about it. I would also have all chargers, hunters, and hacks regularly taught to swim. It is an accomplishment very easily taught and learnt, but the majority of horses, though they are good swimmers by nature, are very nervous at getting into deep water for the first time; and as a very slight touch to the bridle will then make them rear over, it is no joke. Look out for a place easy to get down into the water, easy to get out of on the other side, and where he will have only a short way to swim in the middle; and manage that it shall be on the way home, if possible. Keep his head straight by directing him with your hand or whip; when once he is off his legs and swimming, it is best to avoid as much as possible touching the reins, a very slight pull is apt to bring him back over with you; and for the first lesson it may be well to cross your stirrups over his withers, or to ride barebacked. If you can get a lead, most horses will follow without further fuss. I once had a horse actually fond of swimming; a very unusual thing. I used often to get on him in bathing costume and ride him into a pond or river, and he would swim about like a Newfoundland dog under me, nuzzling his head into the water with delight; and when we came out he would give a neigh, and jump about with sheer exuberance of spirits after his bath.

To teach tricks requires spare time and patience, but is not very difficult with sensible and good-tempered horses; and the teaching tends of course to develop their intelligence, and may add to one's pleasure in their companionship. To teach a horse to fetch and carry, use a small basket you have accustomed him to eat corn out of occasionally, drop it on the ground and say "fetch it." He will most likely commence mouthing it as a matter of course for the corn, but teach him and make him to lift it up in his mouth, and as soon as he does this, even a little way, take it from him and reward him; then throw it a little further off, and saying "fetch it" as before; make him bring it to you by prompting him to come with a leading-rein; then take him out with a long leading-rein and practice the same, making him, by a threat of your whip if necessary, go after the basket—or what is better, a white cloth with oats and sugar tied in it—and bring it to you; always rewarding him well when brought. A clever horse will after a little while not need the rein in hand, but start off at once when bidden to pick up and bring you the basket or handkerchief. By tapping a horse's foreleg with your hand, telling him at the same time to "shake hands," and showing him what to do by lifting up his leg into your hand, and always rewarding him afterwards, a good-tempered clever horse will learn to " shake hands" almost as soon as a dog. Most of my horses would shake hands with me directly I put out my hand for them and said " shake hands," after they had been a week or so in my stable. To teach a horse to lie down, put knee-caps on him and take him to a soft place and secure from interruption; stand in front of him, and telling him to " lie down," tap him across the shins with a cane; this is painful, and he will after a little tapping shrink so quickly as to drop on his knees for a moment; the instant he goes on his knees reward him and make much of him, and gradually by repetition get him to let you keep him on his knees for a minute or so to be rewarded in that position. He will after a few lessons learn to drop on his knees as soon as you offer to touch his shins with the cane on your telling him to "lie down." When you have got him thus to drop on his knees by signal, and to stay there, for the next lessons strap up one foreleg on Rarey's plan, and now make him " lie down" as before; reward him there; and then, holding the bridle close by the snaffle, take him well by the head, and again telling him to " lie down," push with all your weight against his withers and force him down from you on his side. If he fights against going down on his side and struggles up again, you must firmly and patiently persevere until he is tired out and yields; in most cases, however, he will make but little obstinate resistance, and as soon as you have fairly got him down on his side he will lie perfectly prostrate and still, like a "Rarey-fied" horse; then make much of him, unhamper him and let him get up, and reward him well as soon as he is up. After a few lessons you will not need to strap up his leg. A slight pull round of his head and push on the shoulder will make him obey your order to "lie down" as soon as you have got him on his knees. My dear horse "Caliph" I taught in this way to lie down for me as steady as any horse at Astley's, with wonderfully little trouble, but he was an exceptionally good pupil. To lie down thus when ordered might often be a really useful accomplishment for a charger, to be under cover from fire, or for an ambush enterprise.

To make a horse steady under fire, the best beginning is to fire a pistol as the feeding signal; let him get to know and look for the sound, which he soon will get to do and to acknowledge with a neigh, as his dinner call; then let him see the flash. When he has got to like the sight and sound of the gun or pistol report as the sign of his corn coming, fire off his back; then get off and fire across over his neck, under his belly, over his back, &c.; always rewarding him after the shot. Then prepare a bit of ground by hammering in three or four pegs at different places with rings on them, and put a **T** at the middle of your bridle-rein; ride up now to where you know one of the pegs are (the less visible it is of course the better), dismount, and taking the reins over your horse's head pass the **T** quickly and cleverly through the ring in the peg; go a few paces to the front, fire, then come back and reward your horse; mount him, and repeat the same manœuvre at another peg; he will soon learn to stand quite steady and wait for you on your merely drawing the reins over his head after dismounting, just as if the peg was there, as I suppose he fancies it is. I am indebted for this hint to Captain Nolan's capital little book on training remount horses, now long out of print; but I have frequently practised it with my own horses with perfect success. The way of teaching a horse to lie down I bought from a circus rider, and have also successfully practised it myself. I must add that I have known some few horses which could not be made to stand fire; they would refuse their corn day after day from sheer nervous fright at the firing of a pistol.

To *cure* a horse of tricks cannot be taught on paper: good temper, a good seat, and good hands are the three essential requisites; and if you have these, it is probable you know all that is worth telling you. A horse that is a determined runaway I would not advise the best rider to have anything to do with, let him be relegated to harness, where mechanical means can be used to stop him speedily. For shying, patiently but firmly and without humbugging or fuss, make your horse see and smell the thing he shies at; where it is not from mere play, the shying is in most cases fright from ignorance and wonder, not cowardice or vice; knowledge and experience by sight and smell will generally soon cure the trick; provided of course there is nothing wrong with the eyes. Kicking, an ordinarily good horseman will not trouble his head about much; a good chuck with the bit and a cut with the whip on his shoulder is the best punishment, keeping the horse's head well up is the best preventive. Rearing is not the dangerous vice it looks; if the reins are not pulled, unless a horse is weak in the loins or hocks, he will hardly ever come over backwards; beware of holding on by the reins, but catch hold of the mane (which is quite allowable in a case of rearing), and as far forward as possible, so as to throw all the weight you can on his forehand. A horse should be well punished for rearing, if you are quite sure it is from wickedness, and not caused by his mouth being too tender for the bit. A rearing horse should be ridden with a martingale; and if ridden with double bits it should be on the curb rein; not on the snaffle, as is the usual plan. I have heard, and apparently on reliable authority, of one man curing a horse effectually of rearing at once and for ever, by mounting him with a bottle of water in his hand and breaking it smash over his head as he reared up; and of another who mounted with a heavy short club-stick and felled the horse when he reared up by a blow between the ears, like an ox; in this latter case the horse fell stunned, and his rider had some difficulty in getting clear of him, but I was told that the cure was effectual; the remedy, however, seems rather a desperate one.

"Buck-jumping," like what we hear of in Australian horses chiefly, is a vice which like running away I would simply decline having anything to do with if I could avoid it. Though I have once or twice been "bucked" off horses of my own, I have never had a confirmed "buck-jumper," nor would I attempt to ride one; but I have seen several; and some fairly sat and conquered by sheer good riding. One instance I particularly remember. The horse was a powerful, about three-quarters bred, fine Waler colt; the rider was a Scotchman, but brought up from childhood in Australia, and had accompanied several batches of young horses to Calcutta and Bombay. This horse with a man at his head made no particular objection to being mounted, but the instant his head was let go, he jumped off in a canter, and before he had gone half-a-dozen strides the rider was shot clean over his head, without a chance for himself. He did not lose his reins, however; picked himself up in a moment, and said, smiling, it was the first fair fall he had encountered for years past, and that he should not have been thrown now but for the colt's head having been let go in too great hurry, before he was quite ready for him. The young man got on again directly, the colt being well held this time. As soon as he gave the word to let go, and pressed the colt forward, the buck-jumping commenced again. It was really marvellous how the man kept his seat; he was not only not thrown now, but he hardly moved in his seat; and except when he took his opportunity to give the horse a punishing stroke on the flank with his cutting whip, he sat perfectly quiet and still; it was a fine exhibition of horsemanship. He rode with rather long stirrups, his feet well home in them, and rather forward; he had his saddle padded a good deal higher than usual in front of his knees; and he used a strong twisted snaffle-bit with two reins, which he pulled hard upon all the time. He fairly conquered the horse in a few minutes, and rode him round and round the yard at a nice canter, and trot, and over a bar jump, as pleasantly as a lady's hack. Another exhibition of buck-jumping I remember was of a very different description. It was a chestnut thoroughbred, a Waler, taking his preliminary canter at a race-meeting. As he came past where I was standing, he suddenly, instantaneously, almost too suddenly to be seen, dropped his head and raised his quarters, and his rider, an Englishman and professional jockey, was sent flying a clean somersault over his head; I can really only compare it to a ball shot from a catapult; the jockey had no chance, he was sent spinning away and fell on his back several feet ahead. The horse gave a little neigh of self-congratulation, and trotted quietly into the enclosure by the side of the course. From carefully watching the thing, I am convinced the fatal point of it is the sudden combination of the dropping down of the head, absolutely almost to the ground, with the high rumping up of the quarters at the same moment; the whole forehand of the horse suddenly vanishes as it seems from before the rider, who finds himself on the edge of a precipice in front expressly to be shot over from behind. If you can keep the horse's head up, you are all right, comparatively speaking. I should therefore suggest, as the best way of tackling a known buck-jumper, always to put into his mouth, in addition to your usual riding bits, a very fine racing snaffle with its rein (which should of course be a strong one) knotted short to his neck; the slack end to be held in hand. The horse would not feel this to annoy him in any way unless he tried the getting his head down, in which case it would effectually stop his little game, and he would find himself baffled; he would have his own neck to pull against, instead of the rider's hands. I may mention I have often successfully used this plan of spare knotted rein with hard pulling horses; it is a wonderful help and rest to the hands. I got the hint originally from a first-rate horseman whether after a hog in India or with hounds in Gloucestershire, the late General Sir Henry Roberts. I will not attempt to go into the subject of training horses for racing; it is altogether beyond my present purpose. But I cannot avoid noticing a most strange mistake put forth in a most useful and practical little book in its way, called "The Griffin's Aide-de-camp," which says, you should train a horse with as nearly as possible the weight he will have to carry in his race. Whatever may be the weight he will have to carry, *train with the very lightest weight you can possibly put on his back;* a very few pounds' weight will make a considerable difference in the length of his stride, which will soon be perceptibly shortened accordingly. Let me finish this chapter by making my readers a present of what a friend of mine, answering an ingeniously worded advertisement, paid half-a-sovereign for. It was headed "Bonâ fide; no humbug: the whole art of riding taught for 10s. . . ." The return for the money which my friend was goose enough to send, was the following piece of advice :—

"Your head and your heart keep up;
Your hands and your heels keep down;
Your legs keep close to your horse's sides,
Your elbows close to your own."

Easier said than done, of course; but positively nothing could well be *said* better on the subject! I believe the lines are supposed to be a poetical utterance of the famous Sam Chiffney.

CHAPTER III.

SADDLERY AND HARNESS.

I HAVE in my time spent a good deal of trouble and money over saddles and bridles of various descriptions, but on the whole I do not think there is much room or need for much of new invention in these matters. A good saddler will generally turn you out as good a saddle for yourself and for your horse as anything you are likely to invent. I think, however, generally speaking, that saddles are unnecessarily heavy; saddlers always recommend one not to order a light saddle; but a saddle can be made large enough and strong enough for all purposes for men riding not over twelve stone or so without its weighing more than eight pounds. I remember my old friend, Mr. Garden, of Piccadilly, earnestly begging me not to take a saddle under ten pounds, as the very lowest weight he could recommend; but the best saddle I ever had was one of his which weighed barely eight pounds; it gave me plenty of room to sit in, fitted almost any horse, and lasted as long as any saddle could. The great points to be careful about are, that the tree is wide enough in the front fork not to pinch the shoulders, but not so wide as to let the saddle down right down on to the withers; and that the seat is *long* enough to sit in comfortably, and to spread the weight to some extent over the horse's back. It is curious how fashion tyrannizes in saddlery, as in everything else; arge saddles, small saddles, heavy stirrup irons, light ones, padded flaps, flaps without any padding at all, each in turn are patronized. Provided you have the requisite strength and size, the lighter everything you put on the horse the better; weight makes all the difference in the world to him. I prefer slightly padded flaps myself; and to sit a " buck-jumping" horse high pads in front of the knees are a great help; they are also a great protection to the knees in riding through forests. But so good a horseman and so clever a writer as Sir Francis Head must needs fall so in love with the fashion for perfectly plain flaps, as to talk in his pleasant book, "The Horse and his Rider," the exceeding nonsense of padded flaps *straining a man's thighs!* For girths, the best and safest girth, beyond all question, is the "Fitz-William," a broad girth, with two buckles, with a narrower one buckle girth passing through keepers over it. I wonder it has not been universally adopted. The broad girth is, however, I think generally made a little too broad; and girths should always be undyed; the dark colour looks neat, but the dye rots the girthing. What is called the

"Cape girth," a leather girth cut into several plaited strips, and with two buckles, is a very serviceable girth; and though it looks as if it were likely to cut the horse, it really often suits horses which are liable to be galled by the ordinary girths; it must of course be kept soft with grease. For bridles, I think the best for all riding purposes will be found to be a plain double bridle; the snaffle made with half cheeks; that is, the lower cheek cut off, as it is apt to catch in the lip-strap or curb-chain; the upper cheek fitting into a loop on the headstall, which keeps it nicely in its place; the curb, instead of the curved "port" in the middle of the mouthpiece, should be made with a mouthpiece, slightly arched nearly from end to end, as driving bits often are, the curve being far preferable to the straight and unnecessarily heavy mouthpiece so much in vogue, and it should always be smooth, not ribbed or twisted; and the cheeks, instead of being welded to the mouthpiece, should run through the ends of it (without being in any way diminished in calibre for this purpose), so as to play up and down for half an inch or so. This is a strong construction, and pleasant both to the horse's mouth and the rider's, or driver's, hand. I know some good horsemen object to this construction on the ground that the self-acting movement of the bit nullifies to a certain extent the play and power of a fine hand on the horse's mouth; but fine hands are comparatively very rare; and I base my recommendation on a long and varied experience. The "Pelham" looks well on a nice-headed horse, and is a pleasant bit enough for a good mouth; but it is rather a foolish sort of bit to my thinking; meant as a compromise between the severity of the curb and the want of power in the snaffle, it is really less powerful than a properly used snaffle to stop a horse. The "Hanoverian Pelham," or "Bentinck" bit, is quite as powerful, if not more so, than the common curb, if used on the curb-rein; and some horses, if not properly broken, will be found to ride more kindly with this bit than with the common curb and snaffle; but the bearings of the numerous joints in it soon get worn and loose, it then gets to hang badly in the mouth, and may cut the horse's tongue or lips. The "ring snaffle," used from time immemorial in the East, now apparently so fashionable as a driving bit, is not a favourite of mine. It has the advantage of lying as easy as a common snaffle in the horse's mouth, while the direct pull on it through the rings makes it much more powerful; but it is apt in careless hands to cut the corners of the mouth, and it always strikes me as an *unbecoming* bit, it does not set a horse off well. For a horse having the troublesome trick of catching the cheek of the bit in his mouth, the best construction is to have the cheek *ending* in a circle, about two inches diameter, with cross bars through it at right angles; the reins to be buckled into the lower or upper quarters of the circle to suit the horse's mouth. The usual ring-cheek leaves an end which a horse can catch at, and he may be tempted to be putting his tongue through the ring; but the above bit gives no hold for mouth, lips, or tongue to catch or play with. The curb-chain should always be tolerably broad, not narrow, which is very apt to gall; and if the horse is a puller and difficult to hold, let the curb-chain be laid not quite smooth but with a twist or two in the rings; I have frequently found hard-pulling horses yield more readily to this than to any other contrivance. The famous sportsman, Mr. Assheton Smith, is said, when once given a notorious puller for a mount, to have quietly taken off the curb-chain and put it into his pocket before getting up, and to his friend's astonishment found no difficulty in holding the horse without it. But he was altogether an exceptional horseman, and few could venture to follow his example in this sort of proceeding. A good *military* saddle seems to be considered an almost hopeless desideratum; but I confess to thinking that the hopeless part of the business is less in the sort of saddle than in getting the necessary care paid to the saddling. I should be very glad indeed to get rid of the valise, which adds a stone of dead weight, and necessitates a high cantle to hold it up from the horse's back; but still I must say I have seen a Cavalry regiment with the present "Nolan" saddle, after marching several hundred miles on end, with their valises packed and carrying complete marching-order gear, arrive at their destination with the horses in excellent condition, and with hardly any sore backs, certainly not two per cent. But in this instance the officers commanding troops paid most constant and careful attention to their horses' backs, the stuffing of their saddles, the greasing of their leathern girths, and so forth ; and this care, which is so absolutely essential, is, I fear, difficult to secure. The "Nolan" bridle is suitable enough too, but the bits are horribly heavy ; they should be made of better steel and much lighter ; and all bits should be buckled not sewn to the reins and headstall ; the sewing is supposed to look neat and is, I believe, the fashion, but it is a most foolish fashion, whether for military or common use. A "numnah" ("numdah" is the proper word) is, I consider, a most useful addition to the saddle. Not that a good saddle ought to require anything under it to prevent its galling so long as it is in good condition ; but because a "numnah" is the best preserver and protector of the good condition of the stuffing of the saddle ; and it is far easier to keep in order, to be dried after a sweat, and so forth, than the saddle itself. Ladies' saddles are, like men's, generally speaking, made I think somewhat unnecessarily large and heavy ; the pummel and the pummel-crutch are generally unnecessarily high ; and the third crutch, which is doubtless a great help, is generally placed a little too high up to be quite all the help it should be.

SADDLERY AND HARNESS.

The front edge of the pummel-crutch should be nicely rounded downwards, so as not to cut the thigh when pressed down to hold on by. For a lady's stirrup I much prefer the old-fashioned shoe or slipper shape, going the whole length of the foot, I believe it to be the safest and most comfortable; but it seems completely gone out of fashion now. I have often thought, and I here beg to suggest, that for small establishments where economy is all important, a saddle might advantageously be made to admit of the pummel-crutch being screwed on and off (as the third crutch which is not an absolute necessity is), when required for a female or for a male rider; the second saddle might be made a very useful article in this way. Martingales, whether standing or running pattern, I have a great objection to unless absolutely required, as for race riding with a snaffle, or for a rearing horse, or for what is called a "stargazer"; if a horse tosses his head up too much to be pleasant or safe, passing the reins through a plain running ring will generally be found to effect all the purpose of a martingale with far less hamper.

For harness, I have little I care much to say, except to add my poor protest to the many able but, as it seems, sadly fruitless protests already published against the senseless and cruel continuance of blinkers and bearing-reins. It used to be said that blinkers were necessary to save horses from being frightened at the carriage following them; but there can hardly be a more frightening thing for a horse to have behind him than a gun-carriage and its limber, and blinkers have long ago been abolished in our Artillery with the best effect. I have seen it argued, too, by apparently experienced horsemen, that without blinkers horses instead of working evenly and regularly will keep watching the driver's whip hand, and work by fits or starts as they see it raised or down. I do not think this would happen with an ordinarily decent driver and ordinarily decent horses; but if the argument is a good one, it ought to apply not only to driving but to riding, where a horse can see so much more of the whip hand: moreover if *seeing* the whip hand raised has precisely the same effect as *feeling* the whip, the argument seems to tell infinitely more in favour of abolishing blinkers than for the continuance of these absurd semi-blinding appendages. As for the bearing-rein, the Society for the Prevention of Cruelty to Animals should petition for an Act of Parliament against it; the suffering, the utterly needless suffering, the senseless waste of power, caused by the detestable bearing-rein, can really hardly be exaggerated, or indeed sufficiently condemned; it is of course most painful and causes most loss of power with poor heavily laden cart horses, but it is quite bad enough with carriage horses; and one can hardly expect the carter to set the example, though he will doubtless speedily follow it when set, as it should be, by his betters. The crass stupidity in this matter is really very disgraceful in these days of the schoolmaster abroad. "Oh, sir, er would come down on er knees if er 'adn't that rein to keep er up," is the usual sapient reply one gets to an entreaty to loosen the bearing-rein of a poor cart horse painfully tugging against a heavy load up a hill. "Oh, sir, they works all the better with their heads well up," is the equally sapient reply of the equally but less excusably ignorant coachman. It would seem almost impertinent, but it really seems necessary, to point out the absurdity of keeping a horse or anything else from falling down by tying it up *to itself;* and every good horseman knows that the right way to help a horse out of a difficulty is to give him his head free; but still this holding-up idea prevails to an astonishing extent, and among people who really should be ashamed of such a theory. Not very long ago I saw a letter from a noble lord, one of the best whips in the kingdom, declining to support in any way Mr. Flower,* the well-known able and generous advocate against bearing-reins, saying that he always used them himself and always should, and that he believed he owed his life on one occasion to the bearing-rein, which saved him from being pulled off the coach-box when a wheeler

* I would beg to recommend for perusal on this point Mr. Flower's pamphlet, "Bits and Bearing-reins, and Horses and Harness," published by Cassell, Petter, and Galpin. Price One Shilling.

suddenly fell. The noble writer further said, by way of a clincher, that he could show Mr. Flower four horses whom no one in England would or could drive without bearing-reins. It is really sad to think of an educated gentleman and highly accomplished horseman allowing himself to write in such very poor style. As for his arguments, they are simply contemptible. If this nobleman had been able to say the bearing-rein had prevented his wheeler from falling down, there would of course be some point in his story; but as this was not and could not be the case, his being not pulled off the coach-box was due and due only to his admirable seat on the box and consummate handling of the reins; it was the sudden fall of the horse which endangered his being pulled off the box, having escaped that he was safe enough. And as for there being horses that cannot be driven without bearing-reins, of course there are; *exceptis excipiendis;* for that matter I could bring together four horses whom it would not be safe to drive without muzzles on. It is, however, of course, as I said before, with cart horses that the greatest suffering is caused by these reins. Just watch the painful efforts a horse vainly makes to get his full weight into the collar while his poor head is kept up by the bearing-rein, which is moreover generally fastened to the collar so that each effort to get his head down displaces at same time the collar from its proper drawing position; see the corner of the

SADDLERY AND HARNESS.

horse's mouth often deeply cut by the bit in these efforts; and now loosen the bearing-rein and see the difference! The horse can now without fear of hurting his mouth get his head well down and throw his weight fairly down into the collar against his load, and away goes the cart after him up the hill in another fashion altogether. The silly semi-blinding blinkers and cruel bearing-reins, and I may add the horribly heavy and complicated bits often seen annoying the most fashionably appointed carriage horses, are not continued through any fault of our saddlers, who know perfectly well the things should have been abolished long ago; it is the fault of the horse-owners, the masters and mistresses, who from lazy want of will, or want of thought—I am unwilling to say or think want of heart—allow ignorant carters and over-fed flunky coachmen to dictate according to their long-established stupid prejudices. To end somewhat more pleasantly on this subject, let me say how delighted I was to see Lord Londesborough driving his four beautiful browns, all stepping up in perfect form to their bits, without bearing-reins; and that I have been delighted too, as doubtless numerous other observers have been, to see the magnificent horses in the employ of the Midland Railway Company, who in this as in many other respects set an example most worthy to be followed, all working and with unmistakable ease and comfort, without bearing-reins or blinkers.

Great care should be paid to the fitting of the collar; it is frequently not quite long enough for the horse, and it then presses on his windpipe if he has anything of a pull. I do not know why the mat collars are not more patronized; they are half the weight and half the price, and except against very heavy weights must be far more comfortable for the horse. I imagine they are found not to last long enough on account of the lining getting rotted through by the horse's sweat, and from the trace-tug on the harness wearing through the matting; a bit of numnah cut out in the shape of the collar and worn under it, and always well rubbed and dried after using, would remedy the first objection; and a bit of stout leather sewn on each side where the trace-tug works would remedy the second.

There is an improvement in tug loop for shafts which I have also been surprized at not seeing more used. The shaft can be dropped into the tug at once, as if into an open hook, instead of the having first to back the carriage and then pull it forward again; easy enough with a steady horse, but often a troublesome matter if the horse is not steady, and if one happens to have only a boy for the work.

To properly clean and keep leather soft and in nice order the great secret is to use as little water as possible; and always wipe off sweat at once with a greasy cloth before it has time to dry in. Avoid as

SADDLERY AND HARNESS. 75

much as possible using water at all to leather, use skim milk for cleaning; and when you must use water, never let it dry by itself on the leather, but always wipe it off well with a greasy cloth, finishing off with a clean cloth. The following is a good receipt for "dubbing," or dressing for leather, to keep it pliable and polished; it should be used once a month, or oftener according to weather and work :—

Neat's-foot oil,* half-a-pint; mutton-fat, one ounce; finely chopped soap, one ounce; finely chopped beeswax, one ounce; finely powdered resin, one ounce. Melt the fat and wax and mix thoroughly together, then mix in with them thoroughly the soap and resin, then stir in the oil; keep stirring altogether in a pipkin over a slow fire till thoroughly mixed. This quantity will do for four or five saddles and bridles.

When cooled, rub well into the leather on both sides with the hand, and then leave in the sun, or at some distance from before a fire, for an hour or two. Then rub with a bit of soft rag or flannel until every particle of stickiness is removed. This treatment will preserve your leather appointments wonderfully, and keep them

---

* Neat's-foot oil is very easily and cheaply made. Boil the feet of cattle in a large saucepan of water till the oil is disengaged and floats on the water; then skim the oil off and pour it into a covered vessel into which some shreds of lead have been put, and let it stand till all impurities have settled to the bottom, and the oil is quite clear. Then pour off quietly and keep for use.

pliable and soft. If you are much troubled with rats or mice, it is well worth your while to substitute castor oil for any other description of dressing; it is disagreeable stuff to handle, but it agrees exceedingly well with leather, and vermin will not touch it; every other sort of oil or grease seems an irresistible attraction to them. The addition of a little corrosive sublimate powder to the " dubbing," will of course make it fatal to vermin, but then this is highly objectionable to use in case of cut or sore fingers.

For clothing, I would only say be liberal with it, it is a great aid for keeping your horse in condition. The saddlers turn out exceedingly nice and neat patterns, but the clothes often seem to me somewhat scant in their dimensions, not covering the whole body of the horse. And I like to have the hinder ends of the rug closed for about half the way up, or more, by a piece from about eighteen to about twenty-four inches square, according to the size of the horse, of the same stuff; this keeps the rug from blowing up, and prevents the wind from getting between the hind legs along the belly; it is a much better addition than the usual silly and useless bit of loose binding dangling about a horse's hocks.

CHAPTER IV.

Buying and Selling, &c.

THERE is apparently a sort of general consent that horse sellers are more or less dishonest as a matter of course; and that all is considered fair in horse-dealing, as in war. There is a story—I cannot vouch for the truth of it, but it is characteristic and not improbable —that the excellent old Bishop Daniel Wilson, of Calcutta in a sermon on the eighth commandment enumerating the many not uncommon practices which really and morally were to all intents and purposes stealing, especially noticed horse-dealing, and greatly tickled the congregation by saying that "even my dear old Christian friend the Venerable Archdeacon did not scruple to stick his old Bishop with a most worthless horse!" I do not think myself there is more dishonesty in horse-dealing than in any other trade; and I should say, generally speaking, that it was as easy to find a dealer who would not wilfully sell you an unsound or a bad horse, as one who will not sell you adulterated wine, or many other articles. I am thankful and happy to be able to say I have been fortunate in this respect myself; both in not being cheated, and in being able to sell when I wanted without being tempted in any way to cheat others. I have, of course, sometimes lost money on my horses, but on the whole have rather gained than lost. It is odd how very much peoples' fancies vary in horseflesh as in other things; and the animal you do not like and want to sell is often just what some one else wants to buy; and in this, as in other things, honesty is the best policy after all, even in a business point of view. Always give to others, and insist upon for yourself, a full and fair inspection, and there ought to be no reason for subsequent complaint from either side; although disappointment will of course occasionally come under any circumstances. I would not allow a horse of my own to be bucketted about, by way of trying him, for half the day : nor would I dream of asking such favour for myself. But I would always give, and I would always insist on being given, at least a clear half-hour to look over, or try in saddle or harness, or to do what I pleased with in short, putting of course all unfair tricks out of the question, without interference from the owner. If interfered with, or proper inspection refused, I would decline dealing at once. As regards selling, I may say for myself that I have over and over again said, "I do not like the horse myself, but he was chosen for me by so-and-so, you can read his letter which will tell you what I gave for him, and what other people think of him; pull him to pieces as much as you like for half-an-hour, and show him to whom you like in that time; leave him alone if you do not like him; send the money for him if you do." I have had a great many horses pass through my hands, but, as I said, have rather gained than lost on the whole. Horses that I exceedingly disliked myself have often suited other people very well.

A few minutes even if well used by yourself, and if you are not interfered with, will generally enable you to judge fairly of a horse's temper, mouth, and paces; if he is quiet and pleasant to ride or drive; if he will go up or down a hill kindly; if he shies, or has anything wrong about his eyes; if he stumbles, or is at all tender over stones; if he makes any noise when pressed into a tolerably fast pace; or if he coughs, and if his sides heave regularly or with a sort of spasmodic breathing when you pull up. Always manage if possible to get a look at the horse tolerably early in the day, that is, before he has been out at exercise to fine his legs if they are puffed, or to warm them if they are stiff, or to quiet his temper if he has a faulty one. First get a quiet look at him in his stable; see that he stands firm and fair on all his four legs, without "pointing," or uneasy shifting; that his legs are flat not round, and clean enough for you to see the three divisions clearly marked, inside and outside, shin or shankbone in front, suspensory ligament or needle tendon, back sinew or flexor tendon, and all straight without bulge or enlargement from knees and hocks to fetlocks and feet; that there are no marks of cutting or brushing on his fetlocks, or of speedy-cut inside below his knees, or blemish of any kind on his knees; and that his sides heave regularly in his breathing; then see that he walks freely and truly when led out, before he is trotted; and then if you like the horse and feel tolerably satisfied so far, ask for a quiet trial and private inspection, in which of course you may be assisted by any friend you please. Never be persuaded to buy a horse you do not in some degree fancy yourself; a horse, like a wife, may be exceedingly good, but you will not get on properly together unless there is personal prepossession to start with. And horse dealers, like other dealers, are, of course, not so anxious to part with their best stock as with the sort more likely to hang longer on their hands; and of two, or three, or four horses which the dealer may point out to you as about your price and requirements, the one you yourself most fancy, and which very probably is the one likeliest to suit you best, is often somehow most unluckily said to be in physic that day, or wants shoeing, perhaps; *the others* you are begged to have out, or to have any trial if you wish. Do not be driven from your fancy in this way; say you will rather wait a day till the horse is ready;

or say that a little gentle exercise can surely do the physic, or his feet, no harm; but stick to having out the horse you want. I remember so well my father being manœuvred in this way. Going round a well-known dealer's stables at Coventry, my father, having mentioned the sort of animal he wanted, was directed to three or four horses standing next each other, any one of which, he was told, was likely exactly to answer the conditions required. An honest-looking dark grey was the one at once fancied by my father, but, unfortunately, *he* was in physic, or *of course* he should be had out directly; but the next one—a strawberry roan with a good deal of white about him, a colour not, I fancy, likely to be a favourite with customers— "This one is, if I may advise you, sir, a better horse; I am sure you will like him, if you will see him out, and try him." And so my father did try him; and liked him so much, after driving a few miles on the way home, that he sent back a message to say he would keep him; drove him home, and sent the money for him. The next day or two happened to be wet, and the new purchase was not out of the stable, but the first fine day for a drive he was put into the carriage, when, behold! Mr. Strawberry, would not budge an inch for some time, and at last bolted off with a rush! I had noticed this horse being exercised in a light cart in the morning before we went to the dealer's, and he had doubtless worked off his temper for that day, so as to behave perfectly well as he did upon trial. The dealer was quite right in getting the undesirably coloured one off his hands before the other ones, if he could; but my father should have stuck to his own fancy, and he should have got to the stables earlier in the day, before the horses could have been exercised at anything like work: he would not then have been taken in, as he certainly was.

Horses go so differently in different hands, and sometimes so differently from what we expect, and there are so many books which give minutely detailed descriptions of the points of a horse and hints for choosing one, I do not attempt to play the part of "*caveat emptor.*" I will, however, put down a few hints, which may be useful, from my own tolerably large experience. Look well at a horse's *countenance*. A little crossness does not matter if combined with cleverness, and really good-tempered horses often appear vicious to an inexperienced visitor from the high condition they are kept in, and from the bullying treatment of the grooms; but a vicious *evil* countenance have nothing to do with. I would not buy a horse that was very narrow between the ears, or between the eyes; the first is generally the accompaniment of want of courage; the second of want of sense. Nor would I ever buy a horse that was tied-in below the knee, or that had very flat, large hoofs, or that had not a good girthing place; or that had not tolerably deep back-ribs, that is, the back-ribs well let down, not running up like a greyhound, or like a horse too severely trained for a race. Lengthy and muscular shoulders; and for riding, shoulders laid well sloping back; straight back; round body; broad arched loins; large flat clean knees and hocks; are all important "points" among the many other noteworthy points of a horse for one's choice; but I have known straight-shouldered horses that were capital gallopers and jumpers; I have known excellent horses with hollow backs; and others with sides as flat as boards; and I have known many comparatively light-limbed ones work long and well and carry weight; but I have never known a horse that was *tied-in* below the knee last long at anything like hard work, nor a very flat-footed one; and all the horses I have had or known remarkable for endurance have had deep back-ribs. A horse may be a light carcased one, but if he has not a good girthing place, he is sure to be constantly getting girth-galled. What are called calf-knees, that is, the forepart of the leg making almost an inward angle at the knee, I do not object to, except for jumping; and I believe horses with calf-knees are hardly ever good at jumping; for jumping, too, especially for jumping width, anything faulty about the hocks I have invariably found to be fatal. As regards "soundness," a warrantry of which is made so much of, I must confess I cannot see how, in the present state of the

6 *

law on the subject, any definition can be laid down to be of much practical use, or to be much practical protection to a purchaser. No veterinary surgeon would, I imagine, pass a horse as sound if he discovered a spavin, but it is quite certain a horse may have a largish spavin which may not be any detriment for most kinds of work. A spavin may render a horse almost useless for any pace beyond a walk, and so may a splent; a spavin is generally a more serious matter than a splent, but an almost absurdly exaggerated comparative importance is attached to it; its importance entirely depends on its position. A very small splent touching on the tendon is a serious matter, but a large splent well towards the front of the shankbone, and clear of the tendon, is generally of no consequence whatever beyond the look of it; and it is just the same with a spavin. If it is quite clear of the joint and of the furrow of the hock, in the large majority of cases it is of little or no consequence; and if a horse is no way lame when taken out cold without any previous preparation, it is pretty certain the spavin, if there be one, does not hurt him. What is called "bog" or "blood-spavin," that is, an enlargement of the vein inside the hock, like a windgall, I have a great objection to myself, and believe to be incurable, but for ordinary work, I do not believe it is of much consequence; it generally causes stiffness at first till the horse warms to his work, but, generally speaking, does not seem to affect his powers otherwise for ordinary use. Then, again, are crib-biting and wind-sucking "unsoundness"? I hold they are; they undoubtedly affect the condition and the wind of the horse; but the law on this point is not settled. Then, again, in a case where a man had bought a horse which turned out to be blind, he was denied any remedy, as the judge declared that the law always required an ordinary amount of precaution to be exercised, and would not protect so absolute a disregard of precaution as was involved in buying a blind horse. But I have known many blind horses which, unless you carefully examined them especially as for blindness, nine men out of ten would not notice anything particular about their eyes; and you do not ordinarily expect to have a blind horse shown to you; and if you cannot dispense with precaution, it would seem you may just as well dispense with the warranty. A warranty for soundness or for being quiet to ride and drive is, of course, a certain protection, and may be well to require; but for myself I should not attach much importance to it one way or the other, if only allowed to have what I consider a fair and reasonable inspection of the horse, as I have previously described.

Never be tempted to buy a horse on an advertisement, unless of course advertised by some well-known respectable dealer, or that you are acquainted with the circumstances, but most especially not if it is added "no dealer need apply." In these cases you will generally find no difficulty in getting a warranty given you, but you will also be pretty sure to find that the warranty is of no use when you come to discover the defects in your purchase. As soon as the horse is paid for, the "gentleman" you bought him from will no longer be found or heard of at his then address. I may say, I should never dream of giving a warranty myself, except for quietness.

I may perhaps put in here, what I do not think is generally known, that the best preventive of wind-sucking is a piece of soft cord, or thick narrow tape, passed under the horse's upper lip and over his ears, just tight enough, and no more, to prevent the lips pressing together; this does not interfere with feeding or breathing, but it prevents the required pressure of the upper lip against the lower one, and will generally be found effectual. For crib-biting I believe there is no preventive but what is called a crib-biter's muzzle, which most saddlers have; it has bars wide enough to let a horse feed, but effectually preventing him from being able to grip a manger or bar.

CHAPTER V.

Shoeing.

On the principle I have been trying to adopt of leaving alone what has been fully and well told elsewhere, I leave the books of Mr. Miles, Colonel Fitzwygram, Mr. Fleming, and others, to describe and advocate their respective favourite systems of shoeing. I take leave to think a deal of unnecessary fuss and so-called science is wasted on the subject. The shoe should not be too heavy, as it often is; it should fit perfectly even on the *crust* of the hoof all round; the heels, especially of the fore shoes, should be just long enough and wide enough for the foot to stand firm and level on the ground, and at the same time not long enough for there to be any risk of the hind hoof; the shoe should not press on the *sole* at any point, nor against the heels of the frog : these are the essential points to insist upon. A shoe that fulfils these conditions will answer its purpose, whatever may be the particular fashion or fancy. The "Goodenough" shoe seems much the rage just now, and I am told it answers well; but it seems to me so heavy and clumsy an article, I should not care it to try on anything but a dray horse. The "Charlier" shoe is a mistake. The "Fitzwygram" shoe is a good one enough, and for a horse apt to toe or stumble is undoubtedly an improvement; but it requires a good smith to make it and the nails for it properly, and if not properly made it is worse than other shoes. The make of the toe may often save a stumble, but I cannot endorse the Colonel's reasoning in its favour. He says he turns up the toe because we always find it worn away naturally into this shape by work; by parity of reasoning we ought to buy our new boots with the heels cut down on one side, as they generally get worn so when comfortably old. He attaches, I think, undue importance to his counter-sunk nails. He says, truly enough, that in the common nail, as soon as the head is worn down, it is a simple stub, having nothing to hold on the shoe by; whereas on his principle the nail lasts as long as the shoe. But the head of the common nail cannot wear down faster than the furrow of the common shoe is worn down level to it, and supposing the conditions of make and material being equal, I should say the furrowed shoe lasted for most purposes as long as the Fitzwygram shoe. The chief and great merit, however, of Colonel Fitzwygram's system is in his method of preparing the foot for the shoe, and it is here, after all, that the chief care is required; it is not so much the shoe as the way in which it is put on which is of consequence.

The elaborate paring out, the opening of the heels, the hollowing out the bars, the slicing and shaping of the frog, should all be done away with. What is called *opening out* of the heels is the most certain way of inducing them to wire in, and to bring on contraction. The crust of the hoof should be lowered all round, from one-tenth to one-fifth of an inch, or even more, according to its growth, carrying the drawing-knife right round from one bed to the other; then file the crust level for the shoe with the rasp; pare out the foot just a little at the corners, so as to ensure the shoe resting on the corners of the crust, not on the sole, but for the rest leave the sole of the foot and the frog untouched to scale off, as they will in due course by themselves, only removing any ragged parts. Some books, even Youatt, tell you to pare the sole until it yields to the pressure of your thumb. I hold this to be a mistake. I do not pare the sole at all, except just to remove any part scaling off. It is much simpler and safer to let it scale off itself; and the same holds good of the frog. On no account allow the so-called "opening" of the heels, nor let the knife touch the space between the bars and the frog. Except to shorten the toe, or to smooth jagged edges, the outside of the hoof should not be touched with the rasp at all; the usual rasping all over the hoof necessarily thins, and so weakens it. For most kinds of work, and for not very large horses, five nails for the fore shoes—three on the outer and two on the inner side, and six for the hind shoes, are enough. The nails should be well clenched, and the clenches not subsequently filed clean away, as is often done; and in removing the shoe, the clenches should be properly raised before the nails are extracted, not torn through, breaking away the hoof, as is often the case when the shoe is wrenched off at once. I dislike clips to shoes unless for heavy draft, and believe them to be quite unnecessary; but at any rate I would have them only at the toes, not at the sides. For jumping, calkins on the hind shoes are decidedly a comfort, they give a horse a better foothold on the grass to collect himself for his jump; but they should be very carefully made so as not to alter the level of the foot's standing, and not to prop up the heels ever so much higher than the toes; as one sees unfortunate cart horses so generally but so cruelly and so mistakenly subjected to. One calkin on each hind foot, the right or left heel of each shoe according to the horse's action and wear, the other heel being thickened so as to be level with the calkin, will generally be the best construction. But I would not advocate calkins for ordinary road work. Let the frog with its wedge shape fairly feel the ground; that is the best help to the horse. If your horse brushes or cuts, make the outside edges of his feet slightly lower than the inside; if he "clicks," shorten the toe of the hind foot as much as it will stand, and discontinue the toe clip, if you have it, on the hind shoe.

It is rather hard work, but it is not difficult to learn to shoe a horse, and to many it may at some time or other be a very useful thing to know. In my old hog-hunting days in India I have often shod my own horse, and sometimes (though this I grumbled at) a friend's horse into the bargain. It gave me a sweat; but we should simply have had to knock off sport if I had not been able to do it. I learnt in the farrier's forge of my regiment. Pinchers, rasp, a couple of hammers, a drawing-knife, ready-made shoes and nails, I carried in a handy leather roll; the top of the iron pestle which one's native cook always has for pounding curry-powder, stuck into a cleft of rock or into hard ground, did for my anvil.

CHAPTER VI.

Treatment of Diseases.

On the subject of diseases and their treatment I cannot of course attempt to supersede the strictly professional books; and for the general reader I consider the last edition of Youatt on "The Horse" to be on the whole the most useful book of reference. For the best construction of stables, for the best method of feeding, I would recommend Colonel Fitzwygram's really beautiful book, which goes into all details most fully. Then, too, there is Mr. Sidney's, the beautiful and almost exhaustive book on the horse, lately published by Messrs. Cassell and Co. I must, however, jot down a few hints from my own experience. It ought to be, one would think, the easiest thing in the world to tell where a horse is lame; and it is easy enough generally speaking; but it is sometimes really most puzzling. Over and over again I have seen horses treated for being lame in the shoulder when they were lame in the foot; and I once actually saw a beautiful thoroughbred horse blistered on one of his fore legs for lameness which was undoubtedly caused by a spavin. If a horse is lame in the shoulder, it hurts him chiefly to raise his leg; and so too, generally, with spavin or anything wrong in the hock; if the lameness is in the leg or foot, it hurts him chiefly to press his leg on the ground. If the horse is lame behind there will be comparatively little bobbing of the head, which is raised at each step to relieve the lame fore leg from weight. Then if the horse is lame in the shoulder, or in the hip, or in the hock in most cases, he will drag his toe along the ground; if he does not do this, whatever the groom may say, he is not lame in the *shoulder*. The action of the horse's *head*, therefore, will tell you if he is lame before or behind; the action of his *toe*, if he is lame in the foot or leg, or if higher up. If (what is, however, very rare) no amount of inspection can detect any abnormal local heat or tenderness; no shrinking of the leg when strongly felt or pressed, nor of the foot when hammered upon; throw some cold water simultaneously over both fore or both hind feet; the one which dries soonest will of course be the one in which there is most heat. If the heat is in the foot, wrapping it in a cold wet swab will generally be the treatment; if it is from a prick in shoeing, which you can discover by tapping each nail-head with a hammer and the shrinking when the tender place is touched, the shoe and nails must of course be carefully removed, and a strong solution of bluestone (sulphate of copper) should be injected into the nail hole, as well as the foot being swabbed up in a wet wrapping or poultice. If the heat is in the leg, warm fomentations or cold bandages will generally be the treatment. I have heard many disputes as to which are preferable; and I should say, as a tolerably safe general rule, that for anything the matter with the *foot* always use cold water; and for the *leg*, wherever and so long as there is evidently acute pain use warm fomentations; when or as soon as there is not actual pain on pressure, use cold applications. In fomenting, care should be taken that the water is not *too* hot; hands accustomed to hot water will not mind heat which may positively pain a horse. Have two cloths, one in the water while the other is in both your hands fomenting; as soon as you have fomented each leg requiring it, say for ten minutes about at least, before commencing the next, put on nicely and smoothly and gently a flannel bandage which has been soaked in the warm water and wrung out; and over this wind more loosely a dry cotton bandage, or better still one of oiled silk. This acts almost as a poultice, and is as soothing. A little tincture of arnica sprinkled on the inside of the bandage is often a good addition. For cold bandages, the great point is to keep them really cold by evaporation, keeping them constantly wetted with water cooled with saltpetre, or ice if available. Cotton is the best material for cold bandages, not linen; flannel is the best when fomentation is the treatment, or when dry bandages are used merely to fine the legs. Take care that there are no knots or hems in your bandages; that they are wound smoothly and evenly, each turn overlapping the other about a third of its width; and above all that they are not *tied* too tight; always commence bandaging from below and work upwards; strips of cotton sown at the end of the bandage are softer to tie off with than tape. Bandages should be from about at least four yards long by about three and a-half inches wide; for the outer covering bandage, about two yards long by four inches wide will be long enough; they should be kept tightly and evenly rolled up when properly cleaned and dried after using, the tie-up ends of course inside. Bran is the usual material for poultices, but it acts better when mixed with oatmeal or linseed meal; it should be thoroughly softened with boiling water, or it will get very soon hard and dry; but it should be merely warm when applied. Poultices are often applied too hot for a horse, whose skin will not bear heat so well as a man's; for cleansing unhealthy sores, a little finely powdered charcoal may be sprinkled on the surface of the poultice.

I consider the following ailments should not be met with in a really well-managed stable, supposing your horse was a sound and healthy one to begin with—viz.: cough, gripes or colic, sore back, girth gall, cracked or greasy heels, thrush, sandcrack, corns, mange; but as they are the most common, I will lightly touch upon each of them.

Cough or cold is to be treated much on the same principle as we should treat ourselves; warmer clothing, especially about the head, for which you should have an extra hood on purpose; cooling diet, carrots, bran mashes, &c., and less corn; if the cough is bad, blister the throat; if very bad, blister the upper part of the chest also; if there is running from the nostrils, steam them three or four times a day by hanging on a nosebag half filled with boiled chopped hay and bran. A little addition of nitrous æther will make the vapour still more efficacious. I do not believe much myself in physic for a cough; but if it is needed I believe about the best ball to give is—opium, one drachm;* camphor, one drachm; tartar emetic, half a drachm. Mix with treacle or honey, and give morning and evening; keep the bowels from getting too costive by giving a little green food.

For the slight but husky and half chronic cough, which is often most difficult to get rid of, I believe the best treatment is to rub well daily on the throat some liquid blister immediately before taking out for a good trot or canter. I have known several cases of long standing coughs of a peculiar kind cured in this way. A good liquid blister is made by steeping two ounces

* Camphor is difficult to pound without the addition of a few drops of spirits of wine dropped on it, when it pounds easily.

TREATMENT OF DISEASES. 97

of pounded cantharides in a pint of oil of turpentine for a week, then add a quarter of a pint of common sweet oil. For an ordinary blister, take by weight cantharides one part to lard eight parts.

For colic or gripes, give three full wine-glasses of brandy in a pint of water sweetened with sugar; or from two to three ounces of oil of turpentine beat up (to prevent blistering the throat) with two or three raw eggs, and sweetened with sugar or honey; or about a pint of warm melted butter; or, better than anything else, from one and a-half to three ounces, according to the size of the animal, of laudanum and nitrous ether mixed, equal proportions, in about double the same quantity of water well sweetened with sugar: rub the horse's belly well, and give him a little trot in hand. I always kept a bottle of laudanum and nitrous ether ready mixed by me, and have used it with the best results over and over again. It is equally safe and good to prescribe should you be in doubt whether you have simple colic to deal with or inflammation. The water softened and sweetened with sugar is necessary to prevent the nitrous ether irritating the tongue and throat. It is not very difficult to distinguish a case of inflammation from one of simple colic by the intense redness of the inside of the eyelid when you turn it down, and of the nostril; the clammy coldness of the legs, the distressed breathing, the evidently far severer pain, the increase of pain on being rubbed, which relieves colic. Inflammation of the lungs, which is the most dangerous, is generally distinguishable by the horse keeping persistently standing up, and generally with his fore legs stuck apart, and by his oppressed breathing. In inflammation of the bowels, the horse is constantly down and rolling as in colic, only much more violently. In inflammation of the kidneys, the horse generally stands with his hind legs rather apart, keeps looking at his flanks, shrinks if pressed on the loins, and rolls more slowly and less violently when he goes down. In all cases of inflammation I would bleed at once from three to eight quarts, according to circumstances of size, strength, &c.; and give the above-mentioned laudanum and ether drench every two or three hours. If the symptoms point to inflammation of the lungs, the chest and brisket should be actively blistered. If it is inflammation of the bowels, put a horse-rug folded three or four times thick into a square pad on the horse's belly when he is down, and on this pour some hot water, not boiling of course, but as hot as bearable without actually scalding: for inflammation of the kidneys do this over the loins. And whenever there is costiveness, as is generally the case, it is always well to clyster plentifully with warmed water and common sweet or linseed oil until the bowels are relieved. The legs should be well handrubbed to restore their natural warmth and circulation.

Sore back and girth-galls, *if taken at once*, can generally be speedily cured by a pad well soaked and wetted with cold salt and water, or alum and water. But if the back, instead of cooling down, gets hotter, and the swelling *pits* when pressed with the finger, it will probably required to be poulticed, and opened in due course as an abscess. And if the girth-gall runs into a sore, it may require to be cleansed with a poultice; to be touched lightly with caustic, and then healed with some healing ointment: an ounce of white oxide of zinc to five ounces of lard is as good as most. For cracked or greasy heels eschew water or wet as much as possible; if at all bad, poultice the heels for a day or two to begin with; then touch with a bit of lunar caustic, and rub in the zinc ointment. If a horse is subject to cracked heels, as he may be in cold or winter weather, it is well always to keep his heels soft with the ointment as part of his grooming, taking care to wipe it away clean before going out to exercise so as not to pick up dust; and take care, too, that his heels are always rubbed thoroughly dry after washing them, if washing is necessary, and before the ointment is rubbed in. Colour the ointment with a little finely powdered charcoal for black legs.

For thrush—an offensive discharge from the frog—it is also generally best to poultice to begin with, then dress with a pledget of tow well soaked in tar in which mix a little finely powdered bluestone. Push the

7 *

pledget into the cleft of the frog with a wedge; a fresh dressing daily. It need not interfere with work.

For sand-crack, if it is not a bad one and the horse is not lame with it, carefully wash all dirt out of it, pare down the edges carefully, softening the hoof for this purpose if it is very hard by letting it stand for a quarter of an hour in water, dress the place with the hoof ointment mentioned below, and fortify the hoof by winding round it and tying off tightly, the knot outside of course so as not to catch in action, a piece of strong tape dipped in warm cobblers' wax or glue; and favour the hoof from jar at the part below the crack by scooping out the crust a little to admit a piece of india-rubber just there between it and the shoe, which must be chambered for the purpose. If the crack is a bad one, you must lay the horse up, wash out carefully and fortify the hoof as above, having first injected a strong solution of bluestone into the crack, blister the coronet to promote the growth of healthy horn, and wait till the hoof has grown down and the crack with it; open the binding and dressing after a few days to see that there is no growth of fungus through the crack; should there be such, it must be destroyed with bluestone or caustic, and the dressing and binding renewed. If the crack is actually through the *coronet*, it must be touched there with a hot iron. But if you have good feet to start with and use the hoof ointment as part of the grooming every other day, and keep the hoofs cool and moist, there will not be much fear of sand-crack. For this take :—

Mutton fat, 4 lbs.; wax, $\frac{1}{2}$ lb.; finely powdered resin, $\frac{1}{4}$ lb. : add tar only just enough to colour it. Melt together the fat and wax and thoroughly mix in the resin, in a pipkin over a slow fire. A very little of this to be rubbed, *not smeared* to close the pores and collect the dust, well into the hoofs from the coronet downward. The soles of the feet (not the heels) should always be washed out with cold water daily; and the *frog* should be dressed lightly with tar. Tar is bad for the *hoofs*, which are rendered dry and brittle by it; the more water the hoofs get the better.*

Corns are brought on of course by bad shoeing, the shoe being allowed to press on the sole instead of resting entirely on the crust or outer wall of the hoof; they are often very difficult to get rid of, as ours are. It is best to poultice for a day or two to begin with, then pare out nicely and completely with a fine drawing knife, then dress with a liitle nitric acid, then rub in the hoof ointment, then cover over with tow, and then shoe with leather; the leather not merely under the shoe, but covering the whole sole of the foot.

For mange, I believe the best application is Macdougall's dressing for sheep, if procurable; if not, pound sulphur into a paste with oil of turpentine and

---

* I do not believe in the benefit of "stopping," generally speaking; it so very soon gets hard and dry, and it is then of course worse than useless.

rub well in, having previously well opened the pores of the skin by a good washing with warm soap and water. Wash off after a couple of days with warm soap and water, and renew the dressing if necessary; this you can ascertain partly by the smooth cleanly appearance of the skin, or the contrary; and by rubbing with your nails, which if the horse curls up his lips at and evidently enjoys is a sign he is still itchy. An ounce of carbolic acid, liquid, mixed with a quart of water, is also a good wash for an itching skin; and if the sulphur and turpentine dressing does not seem to answer, substitute carbolic acid, crystals, one ounce, with two ounces of sulphur, pounded into an ointment with six ounces of lard. Butter-milk is an excellent wash for an itchy skin, if it does not seem bad enough to require, or should there be a difficulty about applying the dressing.

For a little ordinary sore or wound, a touch with lunar caustic is generally the best thing; or dabbing with a solution of bluestone; or powdering with a little white oxide of zinc. If the place is itchy but not raw, a little mercurial ointment is frequently most useful. For a tender raw wound, such as a broken knee for instance, the best application in the first instance is the simple solution of gum arabic; it is at once healing, protecting, and painless; a little very finely powdered myrrh or aloes may be mixed with it to keep flies from it. For a wound which should be closed speedily, as a very badly broken knee, or the edges of a vein which has been badly pinned up after bleeding, there is nothing like the touch of a hot iron, the swelling from which brings the edges together; then dress with healing ointment. To aid the healing of sores, cracked heels, &c., a dose of physic is generally the best prescription. Give from four to six and a half drachms of Barbadoes—mind they are Barbadoes—according to the size of your horse, five drachms will generally be sufficient, and two drachms of pounded ginger; make into a ball with honey, treacle, or butter, and a little flour. Starve, by putting on a muzzle, for twelve hours before the ball; take out for a little exercise if possible after giving it; and let the horse have plenty to drink; so treated the physic will work off safely and quickly. If the horse looks yellow, showing the liver is out of order, about the inside of the eyelid and nostril, or pale instead of the usual healthy red, add one drachm of calomel to the dose of physic. To cool the skin, or the legs if swollen, about a table-spoonful of powdered nitre mixed with the feed of corn morning and evening, is a good thing. And if the horse's skin is unhealthily dry and tight to the feel, the same quantity of pounded nitre and black sulphuret of antimony or half a drachm of tartar emetic mixed, given in the same way, will often make a wonderful improvement. For worms, give one drachm of calomel made into a small ball with one drachm of pounded resin and one drachm of ginger before putting on the muzzle to starve for the physic, then the physic ball; and clyster a few times with linseed oil, or three four hours afterwards, before the physic has commenced operating.

For a horse requiring a restorative between the heats of a race or after a severe run, give two wine-glasses of sherry, or one wine-glass of brandy, in a pint of water well sweetened with sugar, adding half an ounce of the laudanum and nitrous ether; or a pint of good ale sweetened with sugar, with the same addition, if at hand. It is well to accustom a horse to take a drench* of this kind; if well sweetened and kindly given he will soon make no objection to it, but quite the contrary; and it is often a great advantage his taking it. In the same way a mouthful of strengthening bread may often be most useful where anything of a feed would be impossible: for this, to one pound of coarse flour add one drachm of opium, one ounce of

---

* The old-fashioned drench-horn was very awkward to use, the big end being difficult to get into the horse's mouth. They are much improved now by being made with wooden stoppers at each end, the fluid passing through the *small* end into the horse's throat. I always used, myself, a common pint bottle with the neck covered with stout leather; out of several bottles I chose for this purpose the one from which I found water flow most freely; there is a great difference in this respect in the necks of bottles. Take care not to give at once more than the horse can swallow at a gulp, removing the drench each time for him to swallow, and not giving the second draught till he has swallowed the first, which you can see by watching his gullet.

TREATMENT OF DISEASES. 105

powdered ginger, two ounces of sugar, and a quarter of an ounce of salt: bake into scons or cakes of handy size to carry, fresh and fresh as wanted, not letting them get too hard or stale.

Some persons have a strange idea that a tired horse should not be let drink until he has eaten something, and the poor brute is thought very bad if he will not eat; but of course the natural thing is for him to take a drink first. If much exhausted, let him have a restorative draught first, or some gruel to begin with, if it is ready; then his water if he will drink it, and then his corn. I would note here that a common cause of gripes or colic is the watering of horses too soon after their feed of corn, instead of before. The water should not, of course, be cold enough to chill, but horses generally have a great dislike to anything like actually warm water. To make gruel, put a pound of oatmeal to a gallon of water, and keep constantly stirring it till it boils, and then till it is nearly cool. Barley meal may be used as a substitute, but it is not nearly as good as oatmeal. A pint measure of meal stirred well into a bucket of water, is a good drink to offer a tired and thirsty horse should gruel not be ready when he comes in. Another strange idea commonly held and advocated is that a tired horse must needs be made to walk about till he is cool. If he wants to keep moving, let him; but if not, let the poor brute stand still; loosen his girths of course, and ease him of hamper as much as you can, thow a rug loosely over him, and let him quietly recover himself a bit, before you do anything else to him.* Horsemen often strangely forget to dismount at a check, or when halting to rest a horse for a few minutes; to relieve him of weight is of course the greatest rest.

It is surely well, and by no means difficult to learn, how to bleed a horse, as well as to shoe him. After being once shown the way a very little practice is sufficient; and use a lancet, not the fleam and bloodstick, which should be abolished as utterly rude instruments. A very broad-shouldered strong abscess lancet, which you can get from the good veterinary instrument-makers (more than half-an-inch wide mine are), is the best to use; held firmly between the thumb and forefinger at the place beyond which the blade should not penetrate, that is, about half-an-inch from the point. For the thigh-vein, and the vein on the face under the eye, from both of which it may sometimes be advisable to bleed, smaller lancets should of course be used. I would not bleed from any other veins; I do not believe

---

* A really tired horse should not be teazed with too much grooming, which is often the cause of his breaking out into a second sweat. But let his legs be well hand-rubbed from arms and thighs to knees and hocks, and from knees and hocks to pasterns. This, like the Eastern shampooing, gives the greatest relief to tired limbs and muscles.

TREATMENT OF DISEASES.

there is any particular advantage in the so-called *local* bleeding from other veins. Bleeding at the toe, which was much in vogue at one time, I object to altogether. Bleeding is, I consider, advisable in all cases of acute inflammation, where some powerful immediate effect is needed, like an emetic in human medicine, to make disease amenable to treatment. But it is far too indiscriminatingly applied. In simple fever cases it is, I am certain, wrong to bleed; a gentle stimulant, such as nitrous ether, in doses of from one and a half to two and a half ounces in twice the quantity of water well sweetened with sugar, two or three times a day, is the best treatment. To close the vein after bleeding, bring the edges of the cut together, without pulling out the skin, and run a small clean pin through them in the middle; over the pin wind and tie in a figure of **8** a little tow, or some hairs from the horse's mane, which must be moistened with blood or they will not tie. Take care that the horse cannot rub the place; and remove the pin after not less than twenty-four hours.

Rowelling—the insertion of a piece of leather or pledget of tar smeared with blistering ointment under the skin—is, I believe, seldom practised nowadays; I think it a stupid operation, merely a rough and painful way of blistering under the skin instead of above it. Setons—the running a tape under the skin—may to a certain degree be put in the same category as rowels, but they are often very useful in tumour cases, and to empty an abscess, when the tape should be dressed with tincture of iodine. I know some veterinary surgeons are very fond of using setons, but for most cases I infinitely prefer a blister. Seton-needles are generally made most unnecessarily large. A common packing-needle is generally large enough.

Firing is, happily, much less commonly inflicted than it used to be, but it is still, I think, practised far too often. The theory of firing is said to be a permanent strengthening of the weakened limb by the contraction of the skin when healed after the operation forming a permanent bandage. But for splents, spavins, or any bony enlargement, the rational treatment is to *loosen* the skin, not to tighten it over the part; wherever, therefore, bone is concerned, firing is wrong. It may, however, sometimes be advantageously used after a strain of the sinews or any ligament, or for curb, and should always be in straight perpendicular lines, no diamond or horizontal fancy patterns; it may, too, be used on occasion in bad cases of inflammation of the bowels or lungs, by way of an immediate and severe blister; and just a touch of the hot iron will sometimes dispose a wound or sore to put on healthy action when other means have failed. Blistering immediately after, and on the top of the firing, is a simply brutal practice, and should never be allowed. Be very careful, before firing or blistering, to remove first all acute heat from the part by cold bandages or similar means; blistering a leg when it is in an inflamed state, or at all hot, is a most serious mistake. Be careful, too, in taking all precautions against blemishing by the horse rubbing himself against post, or stall, &c.; and do not be in a hurry to wash off or remove the cicatrix, soften it with an oiled feather, but let it scale off entirely of itself.

Lampas—a swelling of the front bars of the roof of the mouth to the level—or even above the level of the upper teeth, sometimes keeps a horse from feeding properly; and, if so, should be relieved by cutting with a sharp penknife towards the teeth, then sponged or dabbed with some warm salt and water. I have generally found this give relief at once, like lancing a child's gums; but if a horse is constantly troubled with it, so as often to interfere with his feeding, it is well to lower the enlarged bars with a hot iron, as you would apply caustic to an enlarged tonsil.

Giving a horse a ball requires a good deal of practice, but any good groom ought to know how to do it; the poor horse's tongue is, however, generally handled and pulled with unnecessary roughness; and the balling-iron is generally made most unnecessarily heavy and clumsy, which makes the horse fight more than he otherwise would. I give the dimensions of the balling-iron I have always made to my own order; it is not a circle, but open at one end. In the clear for the hand to pass through, three and a half inches between the mouth-bars, and five inches wide, the ends turned over for an inch or so to prevent slipping out of the mouth, and sloping a little outwards, so as not to hurt the lips; the closed side to be well fitted into a wooden handle about four inches long, also sloping outwards; the scantling to be about four-tenths of an inch of oval wrought steel; all to be very nicely smoothed and polished. I have often used a small stirrup-iron, for want of anything better at hand.

Perhaps I ought to tell how I come to talk so confidently about methods of performing operations. It is a bit of confession, and I hope I may not be thought very cruel, my object being a humane one. Shortly after joining my first regiment, a brother officer asked me to shoot a bay pony which seemed to have something internally wrong about him, as he could not be got into condition; he was a perfect scarecrow to look at, entire, and about six years old. Instead of shooting him, I asked to keep him, and under the kind instructions of our Veterinary Surgeon, used him as my *vile corpus* to experiment upon. Every sort of operation, in turn, did I perform on poor pony; but, strange to say, he thrived on it all most wonderfully; and when I had done with him, I gave him away in capital condition to our Bandmaster, who used him for long afterwards.

I have referred to Colonel Fitzwygram's book about horses, their feed, and stables. He gives a receipt for

TREATMENT OF DISEASES. 111

fattening food, which he says is quite equal to "Thorley's," and which costs only about ten pounds a ton, instead of forty pounds. But I object to anything of the kind for horses, as unnatural and prejudicial to their wind, however good such a method may be for cattle. I should say that, generally speaking, gentlemen's and dealers' horses are too hghly fed; and this high feeding often acts injuriously on their skin, legs and temper. The allowance to our Cavalry horses is from eight to ten pounds of oats, twelve pounds of hay, and eight pounds of straw, daily; thirty-two pounds of hay if oats cannot be given; and one and a-half pound of bran in lieu of one pound of oats. I should say from five to six pounds of corn is sufficient for most horses in ordinary work. Race-horses get from twelve to sixteen pounds; hansom cab horses often eat eighteen pounds of corn in the day; but their life and work is of course exceptional. I think too much importance is attached to the necessity of high corn feeding for work. At the Cape, the horses are ridden long journeys, and at a good pace, and are generally in capital wind, chiefly on grass food with very little corn. To put and keep a horse in good condition, a dose of physic to begin with, good sound oats, neither too much nor too little according to the work he has to do, sound sweet hay, plenty of good grooming to keep his skin and circulation healthy, a good stable, and good clothing, will not need fattening "mixtures," whether for show or for work. But if a little fattening aid is wanted, sugar in all and any of its forms is about the most fattening thing possible, and boiled barley mixed with sugar or molasses will be found as good a mixture as any. And if a horse is weak, and has very much leeway to make up, I would give him a tonic ball to help him. I have found the following a good prescription: gentian, 2 drachms; ginger, 1 drachm; sulphate of iron, 2 drachms: make into a ball with treacle or honey and a little flour, and give once or twice a day, before the morning's exercise or grooming, and before the evening's feed, as he may seem to need it, for a week or so. Carrots are very valuable food, especially for a sick horse; and the addition of a few carrots, sliced, into the feed of corn, will make the horse chew, and consequently digest, his oats better; it is this, indeed, that is the chief advantage of mixing chopped hay, or chaff, or bran, with the oats. Lucern is a most excellent green food, better and far less wasteful than vetches; it is a profitable crop for this purpose, and it is surprising it is not more used. If watered, it will grow again and again after being cut. Barley, though not as good staple food for the horse as oats, agrees very well with him if well crushed; and so does Indian corn; but both need to be well crushed, and should be slightly wetted a little before giving, to soften. Beans are a capital addition to the corn for a horse on a

TREATMENT OF DISEASES.

journey or in hard work, but they also require to be crushed, and should be softened. All corn should be well sifted of the dust before putting into the manger; this dust often causes cough from irritation of the throat.

Regarding stables, I think there is somewhat exaggerated objection made to there being a hayloft over; it is so great a saving and convenience; and if there is, as there ought to be, a ventilating opening (which should have a wire grating to keep birds out) of not less than ten inches diameter for each stall, just below the ceiling, the horse's breath will escape without at all contaminating the hay in the loft, if it is properly floored. There should, too, be always a similar opening for ventilation in each stall, at about fifteen inches from the ground; this is often neglected, and even objected to, from needless fear about cold, but it is essential to procure proper ventilation for the horse when he is lying down, and for draught to make the foul air ascend and escape. Stable doors should not be less than four feet wide by eight feet high, opening outwards, and if possible towards the south; and all edges, both of woodwork and masonry, should be nicely rounded off; and they should not be too dark. Darkness, want of ventilation, and the consequently poisonous ammoniacal fumes, are the most frequent and fertile causes of disease; especially of blindness, and of that terrible plague, glanders. Stalls should never be less than seven feet wide by nine feet long, nor less than twelve feet high; and the slope for drainage should be of the very slightest; the making a horse stand on a slope, as we often see, is a thoughtless piece of cruelty, and is most trying to his legs. Stalls should not be littered in the daytime: the cooler the feet and legs can be kept the better. For bedding, as long as the litter is kept well aired and dry, the older it is the better, both for softness, and not to tempt a greedy horse to eat it. The high manger for hay, forcing a horse to stretch up his head for every mouthful and at the risk of pulling hayseeds into his eyes, is another thoughtless arrangement which should not be seen in any decent stable. The water by the horse in his stable is a good plan, I think; it seems the most natural, and he will drink less, but to better purposes for digestion, than when watered at long intervals. A horse drinks about four gallons of water a day; he should always have soft water if possible.

I am old enough to remember the great controversy between "Nimrod" and others on the advisability, or otherwise, of what was then called "summering" hunters, that is, turning them out to grass at the end of the hunting season. Lawrence, a great authority in those days, advocated it strongly; "Nimrod" was altogether opposed to it; he ridiculed it as simply letting go out all the good you had been at so much pains to get into your horse, and would allow no summering, beyond giving some green food in a loose box. The turning out to grass was and is, I must say, often done in a very unwise, not to say cruel, manner. A horse accustomed to a warm stable, company, and high corn feeding, is turned out, perhaps on a bad day and with unhealed sores from firing or blistering, into a field without shelter of any sort, no company, a poor bite of grass, and a nasty place to water at; under such circumstances, the holiday can hardly be a happy or a healthy one. But under proper conditions, I maintain there is nothing so renovating to a horse all round as a two or three months' run at grass. I bargain, however, for a good comfortable shed to shelter in, with its opening towards the south, good grass, a good watering place, for the first two or three days a feed of corn, no unhealed open sores for flies to madden him, and should the weather be cold he should not be turned out without an old rug of some sort on him to begin with; the outdoors run will then do him good all over, as nothing else can; just as nothing can equal the benefit of a complete change of air, climate, scene, and diet to a hard-worked man wanting recreation and rest.

THE END.

BOOKS PUBLISHED BY
WILLIAM RIDGWAY, 169 PICCADILLY, LONDON, W.

DARVILL'S ENGLISH RACE-HORSE.
In 2 vols. with plates, price 30s. New Edition.
A TREATISE ON THE CARE, TREATMENT, AND TRAINING OF THE ENGLISH RACE-HORSE;
With Important Details applicable to bettering the condition of Horses in general.

By R. DARVILL, V.S. to the Seventh Hussars.

"Never before was such a book written in any language so replete with those minute but indispensable particulars of practice, and by a writer who has personally performed his part throughout the whole of the practice. This is the true book of reference for every stud and training groom, and every jockey."—Vide *Lawrence on the Horse*, p. 297 ; also, *The Sporting Magazine*, and *British Farmers' Magazine.*

THE FARMERS' MEDICAL DICTIONARY FOR THE DISEASES OF ANIMALS.
By CUTHBERT W. JOHNSON, F.R.S.

Price 6s.

"This is a very useful work. It contains a great variety of recipes for the cure of the diseases of domestic animals, which have long been successfully employed in an extensive practice in the south of England."
—*Gardeners' Chronicle.*

"A capital work."—*Mark Lane Express.*

THE IMPROVED SHORTHORN.
Notes and Reflections upon some facts in
SHORTHORN HISTORY,
With remarks upon certain principles of
BREEDING.
By WILLIAM HOUSMAN.

Price 2s.

www.ingramcontent.com/pod-product-compliance
Lightning Source LLC
Chambersburg PA
CBHW021918180426
43199CB00032B/691